"*Words Chosen for the Wall* is a conversation with country, oppressors, a silent God, love, and familia. Harold Recinos punches through the divide with the voice that stands with the wounded human. One moment you are walking along the river and the next on the edge of the earth at Machu Picchu, Recinos leaves no stone unturned in this collection, he throws everything at us, including the kitchen sink."

—Edward Vidaurre
Author of *By Throat, by Miracle: New & Selected Poems*

"Amid prayers, protests, recollections, conjurings, and calls-to-action, *Words Chosen for the Wall* voices the particularities of a future archaeology for a world in ruin, where the wretched of the earth are not only given names but imprinted on public grounds. In this collection, Harold Recinos's poetry knows that the story of the street also tells the story of the 'living and everyone who now mourns.'"

—Christopher Rey Pérez
Author of *gauguin's notebook: a retrospective*

"In *Words Chosen for the Wall*, Harold Recinos sings an urban song of barrio youth who grapple against a nation intent on their destruction, while proudly tagging tenement walls with 'Ora Pro Nobis!' With rhythmic consistency, Recinos hews columnar stanzas that stand like lyrical candlesticks lit for Spanish Mass, like stipes of a bisected crucifix, like love letters inscribed on posts of cedar, pine, or cypress. With an interrogatory spirit and indelible voice, Recinos refines his poetics of Americana, class struggle, and Catholic liberation."

—Diego Báez
Author of *Yaguareté White: Poems*

"Like an archeologist excavating layers in the cartographies of memory, Harold Recinos weaves the reader into piercing stories of childhood and the communal lives of a people who forge life from death and wholeness from the shards of time. The poems of this book are to be contemplated, for they will reveal the world of the poor and of the God who is encountered in the tenements of New York City, in the villages of El Salvador, in the rubble of Gaza, and in every rejected place where holiness has pitched its tent and dwells."

—Leo Guardado
Author of *Church as Sanctuary: Reconstructing Refuge
in an Age of Forced Displacement*

"Thomas Merton states that when people '[live] out of touch with other people they tend to lose that deep sense of spiritual realities which only pure love can give.' In *Words Chosen for the Wall*, Harold Recinos finds God has become elusive in churches oblivious to people's lived realities. Recinos leads us in search for a God sometimes located where the marginalized congregate, where 'herbs from their tiny villages' are the greatest gifts."

—Alma Rosa Alvarez
Author of *Liberation Theology in Chicana/o Literature: Manifestations
of Feminist and Gay Identities*

Words Chosen for the Wall

Words Chosen for the Wall

HAROLD J. RECINOS

RESOURCE *Publications* · Eugene, Oregon

WORDS CHOSEN FOR THE WALL

Resource Publications
An Imprint of Wipf and Stock Publishers
199 W. 8th Ave., Suite 3
Eugene, OR 97401

www.wipfandstock.com

PAPERBACK ISBN: 979-8-3852-2002-1
HARDCOVER ISBN: 979-8-3852-2003-8
EBOOK ISBN: 979-8-3852-2004-5

VERSION NUMBER 071624

CONTENTS

SUPERIOR

you claim to be superior
in thought, goodness and
color of skin. how peculiar
it must be to live history
inside a supreme fallacy that
people like me who have stayed
whole no matter how often
you dangled us from trees or
sliced us to pieces find thousands
of ways to protest to rush the end
of empire's atrocities.

THE ISLANDS

I have lived on two islands
for many years, one with a
tropical sky beneath which
old men pushed out to sea,
another chiseled from steel
and concrete both loud with
the poor's lamenting voices.
I have found on them traces
of suffering shaped by the
Lords of the earth who never
hear the frail wishes of those
they chain and dreadfully hurt.
I have breathed the air of two
islands in neighborhoods that
believe God knows things are
wrong, searched for answers in
the places petitioning for simple
blessings and cursed the world
where the creator of things ends
sentences ordering deportation
for women with braided hair, the
kids with rosaries and young men
who work harder than Adam and
Eve ever believed possible. I have
lived next to walls that have ears
and whispered into them gathered
dreams.

TYRANTS

a republic made by the blood
of the tired poor who suffer and
labor for years with broken backs
has no freedom to impart or light
to overwhelm the darkness in its
corridors of government. the tears
of those not considered will only
go on collecting in puddles as they
have ever since God in big steeple
churches decided not to say a word
to the wretched of the earth who
are not on speaking terms with a
religion lacking love for the stomped,
cursed, tortured, and killed. a republic
that bends its knees to pray to a God
that claps for executioners, the Herodian
thugs nailing the poor to cheap wood
trees, and politicians who eat the hearts
of the crucified with applesauce knows
too little about life and far more about
the tyrants who keep their hands in the
public till.

TREASURE

I love you in
light
of day
    and
      darkest
        night.
I sing your
    name
loud
    enough to
reach
    the
furthest stars,
     when
everything seems
set
  to keep me
     apart
and
    in places
lover's
are
    mysteriously
revealed.

GAZA

with terrifying violence, they
have taken the lives of the
ethically innocent in Gaza by
way of the criminal massacre
of human beings considered less
by their executioners. sadly, on
either side of the conflict God is
called a friend by killers and for
victims a partisan to revenge. now,
no one lifts hosannas to heaven and
dear Jewish friends who lost more
than a few they so deeply loved last
Autumn shake with a weeping not
comforted by prayer. why must the
earth be bloodied? how many times
must it be said that death cannot be
a way of life? when will we know
the hallelujah of life together in real
peace? today, the cries from the middle
east makes the planet tremble with the
news of thousands of Palestinian children,
mothers, elderly, and blameless left dead.
bloody Gaza begs us to know the land
belongs to those created by a God of life
who mourns with the living.

OCTOBER

a mild October chill has
ripened with leaves changing
colors on still trees and crows
calling from branches. little
birds are gossiping beside old
nests, children imagine the
paths to take on Halloween and
every breath we take it seems
stirs the earth beneath us and
nothing bids us weep. we tell
ourselves to root for peace, to
listen to her tireless voice and
look for stretching light. then
again, the Autumn leaves rustling
in the gentle wind asks heaven
are you listening to the sound
of many tongues, the remarks
of different nations, the sorrow
in broken hearts and the pleas
to stop the dread of many who
are never named? tell us God
what is the value of life today
for a Jew, a Palestinian, and the
wretched on your earth?

RIVERS

it is a chilly Autumn afternoon
and the city is stretched from the
Hudson to the East River. in the old
harbor Lady Liberty magically keeps
watch though her flame appears
now to burn away like a church
candle that disappears long before
answered prayers. the day appears
to mean something and it will take
more time than any one of us has
to unravel it.

FINE DAY

the first day came with a
brightness to remember like

tight flower blossoms slowly
opening to the sun. Hector's

father was polishing his new
used rust colored car, Carmela

was pulling a shopping cart on
her way to Westchester Avenue

to pick up what God alone knew,
a group of boys were playing a

game of handball using the Perez
Bodega wall and the weight of

the barrio morning appeared to
be in balance. the government

officials never came to the block
to determine who was poor, not

any of the kids knew they had
little more than dreams, and on

this fine day we sat on the stoop
gossiping about how Father Rossi

drank beer at block parties enjoying
the reaching wind that stroked ever

so gently our sweet dark faces. that
day single-mothers did not wrestle

with private problems, the shadows
were sent to the alleys to be licked

into oblivion by bouncy dogs and
we lived happily in our low rent

Puerto Rican paradise the white city
overlooked.

EVENING

walk with me on this warm
evening down the Avenue
lined with projects reaching
to the East River. kiss the
little kids playing on the
surface of the spiraling earth
with the sounds of laughter
and the precious Spanglish
they speak spilling into the
streets. let us walk until the
sunken heads of old women
who arrived years ago with
profound dreams are raised
and their old-world hearts
beat the cadences buried deep
in us. stroll these boulevards
with me not described in the
poetry books with faded ink
and yellowing pages and see
how love arises like a fresh
legacy from the troubled hearts
of men and women who long
ago wrote on the tenement walls
Oscar Romero Ora Pro Nobis!

AMOR

in the night, I held your hand
on the hill above the ancient
city and a kiss strayed from
you to gently touch my lips
and time no longer mattered.
I gazed into your dark eyes
while listening to little noises
coming from the forest in the
clouds and it seemed like the
love that runs in us had bundled
all the nights of the earth into a
single instant. loving you is a
sweet voyage into which I have
placed my whole self like one
surrenders to the mystery of life
with the certain things it speaks
in the darkest and brightest of
times. with closed eyes, I find
you in dreams without need of
explanation and I am convinced
that you have answered me not
speaking a single word.

DECOLONIAL

I wonder how often God sees
us laughing about disobeying
the foolish thoughts of white
theologians that find nothing
more than faults with the faith
of invisible people in barrios
they never visit. I would like
to know whether Jesus took the
time to pray for the Boricua boy
shot in the back last week on the
corner, for Joey who ended his life
on a rooftop with a needle still in
his seventeen-year-old arm and all
the Brown skinned people who like
the so-called son of God cannot speak
a lick of English. help me to understand
the prayers of the women taking care
of other peoples' children, the fatigued
men cutting grass and shaping gardens
with the weight of families across the
border explaining to them daily their
new way of life. the blood stains in the
barrio turned into words that question
the complicity of Christianity in assuring
the satisfaction of the greed that sailed
across the Ocean to carry out imperial
deeds—your God I must say does not know
everything!

NEW AMERICANS

once the chimney on the old
tenement filled the sky with
black smoke old like the coal
burned in the boiler feed by
Victor's father. the color of
flowers on the fire escapes it
seemed faded, faces entering
the building appeared chained
to the darkness coughed up
from the roof top stack, while
the air was barely clean enough
for us to see the very dreams that
drove a first generation filled by
a hunger for life to sacrifice in an
unwelcoming land. the smoke no
longer chokes the sky over the old
tenement and the truth is the kids
who grew up in that building are
not immigrants, undocumented or
so-called "illegal aliens," they are
new Americans, poorly paid workers,
not criminals, not animals, not invaders,
and the repeatedly wounded human
beings freer than the people in their
birth nation who cannot conjure new
dreams.

CONVERSION

I walked along the river unto
the path with flowering trees,
the early morning scented like
an incensed church, the years
stacked in me drawn by a gentle
fragrance into a moment of
extravagant sublimity. mystery
remains today like the time of
tossing pennies against a tenement
wall in a game of luck or a morning
with friends who are thousands
of miles away in Spanish speaking
lands seated on the banks of the
lake flush with fragranced flowers.
I let prayers ascend to heaven with
tender love for with words they will
tell the story of my people who never
cry in vain.

HEADSTONE

I was born in a city hospital
that has provided care to the
poor, ethnic and immigrant
human beings for nearly 200
years. it is not far from the
East River where I learned
to swim. I arrived a citizen
with a first breath though the
English only crowd denying
me a country calls me a spic
who should be bottled and
floated out to sea. I roamed
the streets tattooing tenement
walls, subways, playgrounds,
and sidewalks speaking of the
beautiful Black and Brown faces
that called me by a real name with
God bigger than the largest mountain
looking down on our neglected piece
of earth. I carry a flag at half mast
in my pocket that reminds me of
the gravestones of family, friends
and nameless dark-skinned human
beings. I admit with so many gone
tears roll down my face more than
prayers leaping from my lips.

LADY

my mother worked two jobs
like a plough ox never with
time for a rest. an expert of
early rising to feed her kids,
late nights before a bedroom
altar on knees to pray and not
complaining about her lot. she
was a twenty-year old with a
stiffened heart, drank often in
the dark, told me broken English
tales, danced sometimes with a
paint faded broomstick and even
played castanets her Barcelonian
father gave her in another life. she
kept a night table drawer with letters
never mailed, did not own a single
photograph of her parents and each
day pretended with a great deal of
pride not to need a thing. my mother
attended Mass with me in tow always
lighting candles to fill her soul, talking
with the heavenly mute to make the long
hour extraordinary and finding time to
ask the Irish priest to bless her Rosary,
again.

MIGRANT CHILD

I did not just cross the
border into my country
naming me a criminal,
animal, illegal and bare
spic. I have family that
traveled the distance of
many miles with dreams,
worked minimum wage
jobs until their last breath,
went to church expecting
replied prayers, danced
and laughed in roach filled
apartments, and were buried
by me in cold north earth.
I did not just cross the border,
English drops from me better
than some speak their names,
Spanish in me is older than
the 13 colonies, and when I
say America dear it is north,
central and south to me. I did
not just cross the border, I sat
on rooftops with a twenty year
old Puerto Rican mother, heard
stories about a WWII Navy ship
an Indian father sailed, wept for
a brother prematurely dead, and
now hold a little sister who went
blind in my country where masses
yearn to live free. I did not just
cross the border, I know a great

deal about the alleys where clothes
are hung like flags, I have heard old
women tell hypnotic tales of loved
ones stolen from their beds by men
in uniform, wept with them for the
disappeared, the raped, the tortured,
and the murdered. I did not just cross
the border, I have worked washing dishes,
mopping floors, tagging garments, making
zippers, cutting flowers, moving furniture,
painting houses, taking care of other people's
children and hard in white schools. I did
not just cross the border, this is the land where
my father, mother and brother perished, the
place where my near exhausted heart still believes
God will fill errant souls with wisdom to make life
together in peace.

THE POOR

the poor have gathered
here for years, noticed
in overcrowded schools,
tenements and storefront
churches with drop out
preachers that dare wreck
reality with their latest kind
of truth. they have entered
the barrio from places miles
away from the border, walked
in Spanish across deserts and
into cities to fleeing into shadows
and living new broken English
dreams. the poor come to tell
overwhelming stories coated
with bloody memories of sharp
lights on swinging rope in places
missing from the language of
judgement. the poor settled here
after waiting too many years for
a turn to speak, mumbling pleas
to the Sacred Mother, and waiting
for a lynched unemployed carpenter
to masquerade as a stranger willing
to meet them on the streets.

TIRED

what gets to me is the all
American story told by the
most notorious and not-yet
struck by lightning imbecile
in the country. I am tired of
the man who lives in distorted
celebrity light, the malodorous
fraud against everything taught
by Christ, the privileged elderly
thick man splitting the country in
two, the poisonous whiner empty
of goodness, and truth. I am at that
certain stage of these last long years
when the bullshit from the man who
is out on bond reminds me of vomit
at the base of bare winter trees that
is perfectly frozen and mocking
a Caravaggio still life. I am tired
about so many mortal eyes unable
to see how dangerous for the world
is the malignant narcissist who paints
a doomsday he alone can help the
world avert. yes, I cannot stomach
so-called Christians led by a bible
selling asshole who thinks he is a
gift from God.

MOON

the moon silent in
the morning dark,
anoints the young
lovers up all night
dreaming. it brushes
their heads like a child's
drifting balloon in the
sky and they cuddle for
hours forgetting sleep.

THE COUNTRY

we live in a country with
people more inclined to ban
books than read them, the Koran
gets burned, Jesus is a white man,
beautiful Black lives rarely see the
arc of history bend toward justice,
undocumented migrants get deported
by the left and right to paradises of
death, rich white men are unaccountable
to law, women of every color are subjected
to the will of pretentious men in power
and what gets coughed up by white supremacist
has apparent validity for God. we live in a country
in which churches pray and sing to sanctify
the evil deeds of wealth, the violence of the
Klan, the message of the Proud Boys, the
seditious dreams of Oath Keepers and the
practices of hate against victims in colors
not white, languages not english and religions
not Christian. we live in a country where the
sick, the wounded and the dead killed by the
gun are ignored by legislators kept by the NRA
so exhaustively tamed. we live in a country that
cannot imagine bread for the hungry and where
most white citizens are unable to confess the
lynched bodies placed in despicable graves.

FLEA MARKET

Sunday he toured the small
Texas towns for yard sales
in search of old clothes, shoes,
scratched toolboxes, lawn art,
and tattered old things placed
out for sale like half-moon
wall hangings someone called
art. the man who migrated to
these parts from Mexico loved
to spend the Sabbath day in the
slant light of morning looking
for items he could take to place
on his saggy table in the Spanish
speaking side of town where he
sets up at the monthly Pulgero
to sell things that lived in white
homes. once he showed me vintage
Coca Cola bottles he picked up in
a tiny town with a Texas twang like
the one held by a white faced Santa
Clause in a Texas mall. for the last few
months, after the Barbie movie, he
looked for a doll not looking like those
on the cover of Elle, and finally found
two with dark hair and Brown skin he
bought from some guy who goes by
Miguel.

AWAKE

come sit with me on the
building steps and whisper
your sweetest dreams so I
can take them with me into
other places to push away
complaints. tell me stories
of your oldest love, days of
embracing with a full moon
above, the beautiful things
you found on the imperfect
tenement cracked stoop, the
thousands of ways you have
found to entertain the gods and
how you manage each day to
move about with peace. tell me
a few things about the exquisite
patience you have for the church
goers who sit in rows reciting dusty
creeds that never touch the broken
streets, then let me share a few tales
of the old days on a distant shore,
the unspeakable suffering of a civil
war, young girls filled with tears and
the woman who wore long hair like
the lengthy walk that brought us to
this city.

SAVIOR, SAVIOR

living on the fifth floor
of the tenement we
went up the dark stairs
to the roof to channel
the God of the helpless
with prayers. we had
lived like faithful Job
arguing each day with
the divine figure that
makes bets with the
devil and only finds
time to answer with a
whirlwind. the night
lights of the city always
offered more comfort
to us than the battered
Saints in the local church
dusted by old women who
spoke no English. this is
life for us after the flood
and with the faith present
in our worrying souls, we have
learned to wait on the savior
who promised a hand.

RETURN

some return to the place
they call home carrying
memories forged by gentle
winds that spread the music
their grandmothers heard to
the places children sat for
long tales. they make their
way back to places imagined
without sadness, unchangeable,
and where ancient wood stoves
burn and send smoke signals to
heaven that put smiles on the
faces of the long gone who still
find ways to linger on earth. some
return with notebooks filled with
stories of the things they have done
over the years, the places where
they have found mercy, new family,
friends, and ways to make culture by
reading books backwards just for the
hell of it. I often wish to return to such
a place, to write the perfect story of
it, to paint names on its walls for eyes
to read them and every tongue from
far and near turn them into the sounds
that give us another reason to break
bread.

THE MASSACRE

there are no flags found where
impenitent soldiers slaughtered
peasants. the memory of these
dead is carried to northern lands by
the poor in flight who left behind
the anthropologists who recovered
ashes in a burned down church. here
no one forgets suffering nor those
across the border who attend advent
season dinner parties and babble over
drinks about the lives and death of
blameless families. my dear friend
who heard her children killed from a
place of hiding said to me American
patriotism is shallow and ignorant of
truth. several times a year, I make my
way to the tiny village tucked in a valley
beneath the hills of Morazán to stand
beside the remains of the innocent who
were slaughtered by soldiers. in that time,
I wonder about God's love in a world
buying peace by slaughtering the poor.

CAMPESINOS

the mountain top has a village
populated by poor Christians who
know too much of suffering days
and martyrs. I can tell you they
say furious prayers that sometimes
reach heaven. they are God's favored
who sweat in fields with calloused
hands studied by anthropologists who
misunderstand their subjects. I sat in
a field one night with campesinos who
chose to forget the tragedy of civil war
and amused themselves sharing Psalms
of a God who takes sides, cuts sugar
cane, picks cotton, harvests coffee beans
and is present in the sacrament offered by
a priest in fields with lots of craters made
by bombs. I have never known a better
place to seek refuge than with the poor
inviting me to rejoice like the prophet
of the God who makes streams in the
desert for us.

SELF-PORTRAIT

on every door frame of the
apartments at 1203 there was
a Mezuzah carefully placed
by Jewish families that never
overused prayers, welcomed
with delicate English words
newly arriving Puerto Rican
neighbors and stayed up late
often on the stoops sometimes
talking about ways they evaded
terror. when a little boy an elderly
Jewish man living in the building
frequently took me with him to a
storefront Temple. the holy space
he said was a place to rest and to
hear about the whereabouts of God
who listens to disquieting stories. I
have not forgotten being led into a
Temple with a presence I sometimes
found in the basement of the Catholic
church reserved for Spanish speaking
parishioners. occasionally, with that old
man, I went to the roof to count stars
I imagined like Abraham, Sarah and
my Jewish maternal grandfather who
fell in love with a Puerto Rican girl.
I must tell you the memory of this
elderly Jew lights darkness.

SACRED MOTHER

when I crossed the whistling
river the sacred Morenita was
already on the other bank full
of love calling me in the common
tongue of the weak. like my Brown
people from a world that weeps,
I was not lost. once across this
Jordan, I ran across the trampled
ancient stones spitting curses at
the bloodying militias that could
not catch me, humming on stolen
soil that is dark like the people in
the villages I love and listening for
the distant beating of drums inviting
Brown humanity to life. I was never
more certain the Sacred Mother
loved by waiting for me on the Holy
hill on Hoe Avenue where breezes from
heaven caressed Black and Brown human
beings no longer white property. today,
I cry for different reasons and keep a hand
in the sepia palm of the kind sacred Mother
who migrated from Tepeyac across rivers
and on God's land.

RESTLESS

the restless waiting is getting
to me like thirst when walking
in a desert. I am aware each
day of the possibility of divine
whispering in my ear, yet meet
silence. no matter how many of
us begin the day with prayer and
singing in the storefront that was
once a barbershop heaven comes
up short and even Moses' tablets
tossed down long tenement steps
just prove unconvincing of any
cosmic truth. I am afraid the local
parish has carried us with promises
no closer to holiness despite the very
careful reading people on the block
have given to the book of stories and
the Word made flesh. I have been
going up the ladder rung after rung,
oxygen is scarcer, faith a little more
crippled and God is absent. today, I
will pause on the tenement steps again
refusing the dark thought groundless
being speaks louder than heaven on
earth.

BROKEN ENGLISH DREAM

holy water has been evaporating
all week in the church hardly
visited by any on Sunday. on the stoop
a couple of Brown boys talk about a
lesson shared about a Baptist preacher
who had a dream about America a land
for the free and brave. they did not say
in class that America for these boys was
the land of the incarcerated, a Dantean
waiting room hate sinks slowly in sand,
a place mothers die and fathers go
missing. the boys and girls in Spanglish
neighborhoods who walked among other
outsiders could hear La Llorona moaning
in the dark voices in them. on the block,
they talked about better days for the broken
English lives.

THE BOTANICA

it was really something the night
your mother took us to the Santero
meeting on Intervale Avenue in the
back room of a Botanica crowded
with people howling for Chango to
do them a favor with a back row of
seats taken by the giddy Puerto Rican
kids from the public school. when the
priestess came out dressed in white,
blowing smoke from an inverted cigar
and doing a barefoot dance to beating
drums, the lot of feelings in me jumped
off the tip of my tongue to holler at the
statues of Saints scattered around the
assembly hall, the old women stretching
their necks out of windows in the building
across the street and Julio who played judo
like his Olympic team Uncle from la Isla
del Encanto who would never be called
All-American. I listened to the large voice
navigating the room nourishing barrio smiles
on the faces of people waiting for miraculous
signs from their African God.

SOLITUDE

I trembled meeting solitude
on the East River walk for the
first time. I whispered to her
there were no tears left in my
fifteen-year-old eyes for they
had fallen without charm to the
ground beneath a fractured bench
that I called home and ignored
by officials in the city. quietly, I
sat into nightfall telling the stars
even bread walks the streets hungry
and speaks fluent Spanglish. often,
I wrote on tenement walls in alleys
with other throwaway kids imagining
a future archeologist would one day
find these messages to document the
voiceless!

THE KNOT

far too many years ago
in what seems another
life, I went to live with a
white family that carried
kindness. I think of the
pastor who picked me up
on the street and introduced
me to Robert Frost. for four
years I lived with them and
now recall learning the delicious
Frost line that poetry begins
with a knot in the throat of
which I have many.

THINGS

you hid in the tenement trash
lift from the men who riddled
the bodies of junkie friends in
the apartment leaving them with
holes giving a view right down
to the linoleum floor. I visited
you in the South Bronx hospital
the night a bullet blew past your
brain leaving your left eye socket
shattered like the brown bodies of
the Puerto Rican kids on the block
cops drop. I found you one Sunday
afternoon wheezing on the stoop with
one lung since the other collapsed after
lead drilled a hole in it leaving you on
the sidewalk nearly dead with widows
standing beside in prayer. I saw cops
drag you down the street in handcuffs
because you dared drink a beer outside
of a brown paper bag. I heard you talk
about Shorty who was falsely arrested
on Southern Boulevard for shoplifting
then killed himself on Rikers Island but
not before writing a letter to his Spanish
speaking mother who descended from
slaves. I was called to a cheap cemetery
to bury you with a small group of friends
wishing you had lasted more days with
at least one Nuyorican dream come true.

THE STEPS

the cool breeze on the
Cathedral steps gave me
a kiss. the morning provided
me a peek into the unbroken
dreams of my beautiful earth
colored people. life is short
though worthy of being made
beautiful.

HARLEM DAYS

this country I carry on my back
makes me take a knee that bends
from the weight of centuries of
hatred tossed about by those fully
pleased with their vulgar ignorance.
I have walked down streets in Spanish
Harlem, gasped for air on the South
Bronx's Grand Concourse, yelled at
God on Avenue D on the Lower East
Side and searched for poems in alleys.
I spent hours on the corner with people
who walked here from Chiapas, San
Salvador, Zacatecas, Lima, Tegucigalpa,
among other parts south. I have cracked
jokes with sisters who skipped to this
side of the tracks from Alabama, brothers
who came here on a bus, and more than a
few who flew in from San Juan, Santo
Domingo, Port-au-Prince, and Senegal.
we call here Harlem, Spanish Harlem,
El barrio and the finest place on earth to
shout Halleluiah in every color demanding
to be heard. in my country, hating is a national
game and gunmen are found in many places,
but the despisers will not end us.

THE MORNING

a new day arrives with bird songs,
the gentle wind moving things on
the sidewalk, the scent of Autumn
soon to thrive, the unfolding roar
of traffic, voices taking walks, no
bang announcing a world end and
time to dream again for fresh solid
things. a new day begins with God
forgiving yesterday's errors, weary
limbs springing with hope in ways
they can, and the rising sun casting
light on thousands of worlds. a new
day is offering the finery of heaven,
the trumpeting love of paradise lost
and the mysteries of refreshed life.
a new day invites us to crave more
light until the dark begs us again to
sleep.

EVENING

like mothers who wandered for
days weeping on the long walk,
evening returns unmasked with
love. it comes like them carrying
baggage unpacked in heads brushed
by the gentle currents of a summer
wind. tonight, faint light bounces
on the petals of flowers, drifts to
wind-blown grass and casts last
minute shadows that entertain the
bobbling heads of Robbins playful
before the dark. I confess even God
would not dare to misuse this time
nor heaven deny the sweet chariots
promised to the forsaken who yearn
to wake in Eden and know hymns
not written in church books. I will
sit to let the evening come like migrant
mothers to deliver me to every traveler's
dream.

SPEECH

the fences on the school yard
keeping us in were decorated
yearly for the Day of the Dead
by mothers glad their kids were
busy on playgrounds and school
with safe things to do. we played
wildly at recess shouting broken
English and whispering prohibited
sentences with other alien tongues
teachers did not wish to hear and
never understood. on the school
side of the fence, we were regularly
told English only and Spanish for
home. I would return to an apartment
after school bursting with beautiful
Spanish syllables. I have a beautiful
tongue used in prayer to make God
notice the Brown and Black boys and
girls who live the perils acted out by
confused white minds.

THE JUNKIE

from the window in the abandoned
tenement with junkies shooting on
the top floor, where no one ever says
good night, he stares at the street only
coming to life after pleasant nods full
of longing for a cleaner needle and
God speaking a few words. there are two
others in the room nodding out next to
a half-filled plastic garbage bag with
personal things. beside another junkie
slumped over on a stained mattress
there is a disability check waiting to
be cashed. no one in the place decided
to live on a painkiller, become a dope
fiend or spend life in the barrio waiting
for the next fix. the junkie den was the
place Lelo died of an overdose. but these
junkies could only confess with needles in
their arms that Lelo must have shot some
good shit.

HANGING OUT

one late Saturday night some
people were talking on the stoop
about work in the factory down
by the highway, living on rice and
beans and making enough money
to leave the city. they gave each
other advice about going into the
world to make dreams come true
like ordering café-con-leche at the
counter of Joey's restaurant where
the old men wear berets and kids eat
flan wearing turtlenecks like in a beat
café. the group of friends wanted a little
more advice so Tito who used to be an
altar boy in a church named after the great
preacher of Antioch said pray loud enough
for God to hear, the drunks to stumble and
to make abuelas laugh.

TOGETHER

after the clock chimed eight, she held
back the fatigue from cutting zippers
all day on an assembly line downtown
to work at home putting glass diamonds
into costume jewelry brooches. paid by
the gross, she worked with her kids to
fill a basket with these trinkets that would
adorn the fine garb of ladies who paraded
Easter bonnets on Fifth Avenue. around
the kitchen table they had conversations
for hours about Spanglish, public school,
the Bible, the Rosary, the Holy Mother,
Huckleberry Finn, derogatory things, the
young boys from the block who died in
wars and the first Catholic president who
was talked about in barbershops, grocery
stores and on barrio stoops. her teenage
boy thought out loud saying the truth is
teachers at P.S. 118 can quote Whitman
all they want but the block is not part
of America. perhaps someday, citizens
will agree with Whitman America is a
place of magnificent variety—we will
wait to see it!

THE CARAVAN

the migrants are a step closer
to the new life whispered along
the way. they are not driven by
religious hate, blinded by power,
submerged in crime or fooled by
political tricksters. they have
crossed land, rivers, mountains,
deserts feeling unsteady in places
without light, aim to settle with the
poor in tenements to spend days in
hard work in the country needing
and loathing them. they fled homes
without looking back, arrive daily to
harvest, labor, and take the blame for
crimes. they wonder why Jesus is in
league with rabid white legislators and
lost cause assholes. the migrant caravan
has grown for weeks with mothers who
lit candles in hollow churches along the
way and prayed to find streets paved with
gold for the wretched the drug cartels use
to make millions so they can party like rich
white imbeciles.

THE GIFT

I met a man who came
to the television park in
old San Juan each night
to watch mysteries and
talk to me about the dark
streets of la Perla. I would
listen to him closely during
commercials and asked once
does the old city have plans
to put up street lights and he
smiled, then reached into a
bag he always carried and
poured a tall shot of rum into
a plastic cup. he looked at the
glass fondly, then transferred the
elixir down his throat, his eyes
were like two mirrors absorbing
images from the lifeless TV then
he said oddly too bad they do not
sell time on the streets. we sat watching
American mystery shows dubbed in
Spanish, church bells rang in the distance
and I thought Jesus lied the day he left
the world full of sins and way too
little faith.

THE MARTYR

the martyr testified by the
hour calling out government
wrongs and raging against acts
of violence flattening the lives
that never tasted manna from
heaven. the martyr faced the
demons of hate, all the mobsters
in leadership, the lynching packs
segregating the nation and loathing
the poor. the martyr moved his tongue
in the name of a Crucified God, never
turned away from pursuing justice,
denounced centuries old ignorance and
the bombs placed in his church could
not silence him. the martyr spoke each
Sunday with love for God's suffering
people, disclosing the meaning of light
and with simple signs represented the land,
villages, mountains, forests, rivers, the
hungry, the poor and those waiting for
answers to prayers. the martyr named
Oscar Romero dreamed of abundant life
with crucified people just like the Baptist
preacher in America named King. the
martyr had a soul full of grace, a heart
filled with truth and love to overcome
evil.

SILENCE

in all my years in the city
waiting for night to yield
suddenly to the morning
light it came ambling to
me this thing called silence
which is beautiful. nothing
compares to the way it leads
you across the sidewalks or
just sits with you on the stoop,
searching. sometimes, it feels
like heaven might even empty
a little something into you to
deepen love. silence is a gracious
morning without language, or
Spanglish playing in my head
and no interrupting thoughts
about an absent God.

THE TRIP

estates stretched for miles,
farmhouses were in the fields
and our eyes strolled to silos
standing on hills. the radio
played music rap that traveled
the world save these small
towns. in this lengthy arcadian
drive, the sun in the sky helped
stars find their way to the
nightfall, my son smiled as
we talked of everything and
nothing. laughter helped me
recall a memory of his first
grade backpack that nearly
covered the length of his back
for a year. at first dark, with
two-hundred miles to go, we
stopped while a cool evening
unfolded and the scent of the
forest gave us peace and a taste
of autumn.

AIRPORT

at Gate D-32 in the Detroit Airport
I open my eyes to a woman wearing
a headscarf with dark patterns who is
sweeping with not a single strand of
hair peeping out and her gentle eyes
seem close to God. she pauses to
daydream I imagine with the things
she calls her own. a bird managed
to enter the terminal and she filled the
station corridor with song that kept
step with rushing passengers and
toddlers climbing on chairs at the
waiting gate. there were four bins
by the departure gate labeled trash,
recycle, newspapers and magazines.
I had an urge to write a brief article
about the frayed patience of travelers
who believe in prayer, but feared the
Muslim lady. my imaginary essay
would say there were no one one-eyed
monsters in the airport though the
flight delay felt like it would take a
decade to get home like Odysseus
to Ithaca. then, the headscarf child
of Allah smiled at me and I could see
she was not bothered by the ignorant
who refused to breathe air full of a
history from which the women could
never be removed.

BAROQUE

there is music unraveled
by strings making hearts
return to lost things. the
inspired violins, talking
cellos, deep violas, wind
filled flutes and light rushed
harpsichords leap from note
to note full of magical secrets
that draw us sweetly into the
ways life imitates a brilliant
Bach fugue. the lofty air in
Baroque composers moved
my Spanglish head across a
rubble field and this sound
delivers me to God's blameless
sight with whom I argue about
broken things.

WAITING ROOM

in the waiting room flipping
the pages of People Magazine
the tall thin junkie would have
been a stately figure in some
other life and not strung out.
unbathed for more than a few
months, clothing crusted by
unpardonable dirt, the broken
English kid came to the hospital
to kick a jones betraying his life
since he turned thirteen. pimps,
pushers, hookers, thieves, single
mothers, the poor, unemployed,
and Santeros telling fortunes have
found ways to rush his veins, while
each day skips like a record playing
a song whose lyrics are not entirely
recalled. before the waiting room,
this mahogany child was in Barbara's
shooting gallery and he overdosed
dope in an unfurnished apartment
full of junkies attached to the only
shepherd they love, heroin. the barrio
plague he survived went by different
names like TNT, Overtime, and Body
Bag but in the waiting room this Brown
boy prayed to find the will to finally go
straight.

ZIP GUN

in the backyard away from
the street with a freshly made
zip gun, no longer too common,
but good enough for a bullet, they
went to shoot. the targets were all
brand names like Colt. 45, Miller
High Life, Budweiser Ale and the
favorite for the Saturday domino
players who always sat in front of
the bodega that learned to speak
Spanish—Schaefer beer! it was
the year Nelson came back from
the Gary Job Corp Center with
stories about the stars at night in
Texas and the Hoe Avenue Peace
Meeting that called for an inter-gang
truce in the South Bronx. it was a time
when kids were never gunned down
in school, in stores, movie houses,
local dance halls, watching the Puerto
Rican Day Parade or during peaceful
Protests considered a presidential
threat. the zip gun would never
defend civil rights, change neglected
lives or visit Saint John's Chrysostom
Church for Easter Mass. the zip gun
would take its place in a cabinet at the
local cop station, while sadly on the
block prayers would be said without
end for the dead!

THE TENEMENT

the old bricks of another
creation have known
times of Spanglish living
for a little more than fifty
years, holding the aches
behind its walls and in the
air the smile of those long
gone. home is what they
started here, the intimacy
of friends, the communion
of families and these many
years quietly carrying them.
they have known occasional
festive moments, the voice
of a hidden God, sometimes
even spirits of unspeakable
simplicity and life downright
as it is. they have lived in hope
for years in this place, waited for
heaven to make more than a few
rounds on earth and for moments
spent in the dark to lighten them
on their way. these old and cracked
bricks know each story though they
are strewn about in the rubble lots
now unable to witness.

THE LETTER

dear Loisaida, I remember the
alphabet streets with its crimes
and misdemeanors, widows dressed
in black, Ukrainian restaurants today
flying solidarity flags, photographs
taken in front of a church preserved
by a hymn about the crossing of
crowded ways, the bowery wino
who owned a corner on Saint Mark's
Place holding a sign seeking funds
for wine research, the undocumented
Japanese dancer with her five-year-old
girl who had a head full of things no one
understood and the Polish priest from
the church next to the building where
the cartoonist landlord lived. I recall
the different mother tongues roaming
the streets, the words that floated in
the air without aid from English, Puerto
Rican, East European, Black, Asian
and white faces always offering more
to drive the rest of the narrow minded
country to shame. dear Loisaida, I do
remember psalms read in church for
those departed for that place Julia's
mother calls, heaven.

THE BACKYARD

we have been in the backyard
peeking over the fence at the
sidewalk where children play
and telling stories to the Saints
placed in corners of a garden.
Saint Francis was blessed by
a local priest in Spanish who
now finds himself in Rome to
train in the rituals of heaven
and a boy plays his guitar with
Mexican sweat dripping on the
earth called mother. I am reminded
today of grass meadows and flowers
cultivated on the rooftops of cities
by anonymous campesinos who make
images of another world with plants
breathing and weeping with them. I
sit next to the youth playing the guitar
so sweetly questioning when God will
toss the world into shape to lift us from
weariness.

FLACO

Flaco has been living at
the East River Park for
eight years drinking away
the memories of thorned
youth and a Spring that
never appears to arrive to
see him start fresh. he loves to
sit on a bench quietly observing
the yellowish-red of a sunset
brushing the tops of scraggly
trees. when the pigeons settle
for sleep, he stays awake observing
rabbits that never left the city
hopping footpaths and river lights
skipping on the banks of the river
water. Spanish tumbles in his head
keeping him entertained for hours
and he often laughs out loud about
some image rising from a sack of
nostalgia in him. tonight, Flaco is
cradled by a favorite bench and drifts
into a gentler time.

MACHU PICCHU

years ago, I climbed to the edge
of the earth to reach Machu Picchu
with Aymara friends and in the thin
Andean air celebrated with a priest
communion paying tribute to the
four directions. we shared ritual
bread with a coca beverage for
the Savior's blood and countless
spirits watched in place of the eyes
in the village. we gathered beside
grooved stone warmed by an aging
sun, could almost hear centuries of
mourning pitched by a silence not
familiar to Europeans, then plunged
into prayers never spoken in church
before passing to each other simple
peace. no one objected to time in that
Holy place of earth.

TODAY

this evening, I am looking back
at the day content not to need a
map to recollect in the spreading
night the way the sun provided
daybreak spots of light for the old
man who walked three dogs on the
pavement still chalked by kids for
hopscotch. today, I smiled hearing
the triumphant laughter of the elderly
couple who still hold hands on morning
walks. today, the scent of the summer
enlivened the air, God's ears I believed
could hear the noisy streets, the storefront
hymns sounded on the sidewalk and the
noisy mothers found their way to places
of rest. it was a perfect day for walking
on water, to let time break into pieces and
for turning troubles over to winged Angels
in love with the city. today, the wind sighed
about worldly illness and mystery arose from
simple things to make the most tired among
us dream.

OLD CHURCH

the old church bells ring
God's favorite hymns for
the neighborhood that lets
faith roam around and drop
with a few words from the
lips of the Catholic school
kids looking for miracles.
more than once, I cursed
God in that Spanish way
familiar to Tita that scolds
the Holy's absence from
the block. you see, Tita had
a way of saying things that
made me believe and enter
the red doors leading into
the old sanctuary where the
dead and martyred continue
living. now, when I hear
church bells it occurs to me
they are making sounds to
makes us lean toward each
other with love.

THE NATION

I have been beaten up on the
streets by cops, maimed by
by America, told by the news
the only way I can exist in
my country is with the label
illegal alien, greaser, or spic.
I speak two languages long
a part of this land, weep in
them, laugh and hope with
them and use them to write
words shouted in barrios from
sea to shining sea that pound
on shut doors and get written
on border walls. when America
sleeps, I stay up nursing open
wounds made by thugs dressed
in Lilly white pressed suits and
I hear in dreams tree branches
creak with ropes swinging the
strange fruit Holiday sings. take
a long look at me, go ahead and
loath me until Jesus comes, and
I will do what I can to save my
country from itself.

THE CART

this man pulled a two-wheel cart
with a chair and shoe shine box
in it to the boulevard. his greying
hair, lips fixed in the direction of the
sidewalk and sad eyes reflected years
of struggle. no one imagined him
wounded years earlier in a Vietnamese
jungle, hanging an old decorated army
jacket in the closet of his single room
home, visiting one day a memorial to
touch the names of fallen friends and
sitting on the stoop with little kids to
sip soda. this man still carried a heart
filled with American wars, objected to
the rising price of bread and woke up this
morning thinking about the island his
mother left in the warming sun singing
about being free. this man on the other
side of Eden, living between here and
nowhere, sees things others plain old
disbelieve.

THE SKIFF

is it time to call the future from
the skiff on the Potomac River?
who will scorch the name of the
formerly elect not least repugnant
for his criminal misdeeds? this is
not you see some banana republic
but here the place where revolution
ended life under tyranny, a nation
that has insisted on moving across
the years closer to its truth, where
we weep for those with dreams of
freedom, equality, democracy and
peace at home and on this shrinking
globe. the nation that will not have
many of us for what we are, how we
talk or love must not keep quiet now
about the purposes of the Star Spangled
Banner and what it means to be a country
indivisible with adjustment. in the future
when the amber waves of grain get picked
up by the wind let it be to carry the vision
of a people that will give back life for
those it took and to slap an orange faced
man to a place where he cannot touch the
weak, the poor, the rule of law and the best
of democracy.

SLEEP

the city has slept another night
giving psalmist time to talk in
dreams. the drowsy sound of
buses rolling down the avenue
enters like a lullaby dark rooms
to open eyes kind to such interruptions
an winged Angels sit on the tenement
rooftops keeping watch with sleepless
abuelas over hard working people.
there is laughter in heaven and one
wonders will it ever be possible for
those who walk the streets. perhaps,
we will stand one day on level ground
delighted by life together with justice
and peace.

WAITING

I have been in the habit
of chatting for too long
with people playing the
role of executioner who
are unaware of just how
sick they are immersed
in a vision of the nation
that perceives only white.
the news print lately is
like the old dusty parcels
of dailies that failed to tell
the story of tyrants and
the institutional disorder
that craftily split Black
and Brown heads in two
in the name of brutality
and a racist God. I was
born and have lived in
dark times, stayed in the
places without furniture
loathers know nothing
about, learned to pray
when a child for days
on end when there was
nothing to eat, been in
jails for the sin of bushy
hair and dark skin and
trembled too many times
when chased to be nailed
to the nearest tree. in this
feeling of exile in my own

country, I have lived waiting
to be carried away by freedom
and treated like a human being
with a place on earth.

THE BOY

he died recently like Joey,
withered like a cut flower,
sadder than the apartments
facing night with off lights,
and alone. he left without
leaving words to save us,
the fluttering pigeons with
flight reminding us of the
whole world the boy loved.
its pouring today flooding
the sidewalks and the old
women are saying it means
he is weeping in heaven to
wash us and free us from
sorrow. in the corner of his
mother's bedroom candles
burn in front of la Virgen de
Guadalupe and we take turns
visiting it to pray and drop
tears for the loss no one can
forget.

HOMECOMING

at fifteen, she heads to her
first homecoming dance to
whispers tossed in the wind
saying you are beautiful. tonight,
she will stitch together the souls
of friends and on a gym floor
dance to hypnotic songs parents
cannot name. she will fasten to
feelings of jubilation with Catholic
school mates who dressed for this
ball to dance the night away. tonight,
she will come home to dry a mum the
boy gave her and keep it in a jar to
show. my girl is older than her first
walk and making her way!

THE BRIDGE

I walked to the middle
of the bridge in the dark
hours of morning when
church bells were too tired
to strike the time. I could
see the lights of the city in
the distance rushing away
the darkness and I confessed
on this bridge with the clouds
moving above the gods love
us. I looked at a torn page
of a calendar taken from
a trouser pocket inked with
places visited, scribbled here
and there with thoughts of the
innocent days when kids played
stick ball for hours and marked
on the last day we gathered. I
made it to the other side of the
bridge not thinking about the
loud panic of prayer expressed
in the little storefront church
on Intervale Avenue feeling the
benediction of a strong wind
and almost heard the voices of
those who had descended into
the earth, unwanted.

KITCHEN SINK

in the apartment sink a
two year old is standing
held by his mother for a
bath. she reaches for a
gourd beaker carried from
her village to the city and
pours water over the boy
that makes him merrily
dance. before the little
angel could even say a full
sentence there was this bath,
music playing on a kitchen
radio, siblings babbling in
the other room, candles burning
on a bedroom altar warming
la Virgen de Guadalupe, and
a young single mother with
unlimited dreams for her young.
she inspects his ears, nails, and
hair as if a baptismal cleansing
then carefully wraps the child,
kisses him and whispers, ya!

THE INNOCENT

he died, a Palestinian
child only six, flesh and
blood driven mercilessly
to final sleep, slaughtered
by an old white man who
in the little boys face and
mother's faith saw only
reasons for hate. here the
child who loved to play
was pitilessly slain like so
many others today in the
distant Holy Land. his
bloodied mother prayed for
peace in the city of a country
she said one had nothing to
fear making Muslim prayers,
belief and the sound of a
non-English name. come
weep with me for Wadea
Al-Fayoume, his family and
kind friends. come weep with
me for the people filled with
hate, the terror of vengeance
and crucified Palestinians who
are not Hamas.

TERROR

in the graveyard where the earth
is watered by tears, we shake our
heads asking how long in prayer,
while soulless gun men care about
making life sickeningly hollow for
us. headlines in the papers scream
about the vicious murders of hundreds
and candles burn with golden flames
at vigils around the world. we catch
chilling stories of babies burning, Jews
beheaded, Palestinian children made
into ashes by U.S. bombs. we plead
to heaven asking when will darkness
turn to light and wicked deeds stop?
when will God's eyes open to see the
suffering, the slain, the maimed, the
mourners on earth who cry for change
and life? in the graveyard those who
weep dream of peace though they
are nearer to believing all the gods are
dead!

THE SLAUGHTER

the clocks for many have
stopped ticking and we are
left confessing time at last
is quite sad. the children
who fell asleep hearing bombs
and guns in their occupied
land, those that live in fear
and insecurely played on
their Palestinian streets have
been incinerated for crimes
against Israel that had nothing
to do with them. the scales tip
away from the full weight of the
Jewish past and ethically innocent
human beings in Palestine who
pay for other's crimes in a globally
stomached system of apartheid are
beaten, tear-gassed and killed even
with prayer. the dark has come to
all of us demanding from open air
graves an end to the slaughter and
cruelty masked as justice. I recall
the besieged Jews in the Warsaw
ghetto had a motto 'to live and die
in dignity.' tell me can it be anything
less for the innocent of an occupied
land?

WORDS

we do things with words
tossed like pennies in kids
street games. some are kind,
others come with shouting,
and many without a sound
in english. I like to use a
slight bit of broken english
to diminish the world that
loathes people like me and
Spanish is good to unmask
the darkness of centuries that
kept my Indian and African
ancestors in chains. I like
words that show me a world
without inferior and superior,
rich and poor, war and greed,
hunger and illness, borders
and hatred. I like words that
do not linger in the courtyards
of despair, do not speak white
supremacy, and declare love
and justice can never only be
said once. I like words that
must be written and lift us
from the ruins of history to a
space occupied by people of
many colors made you see in
the image of God.

THE END

politics is no laughing matter
for those who still have some
hope for democracy, the country
and its people. sadly, there are
citizens who believe living one
more day with freedom will only
make them ill. politics these days
is a thousand nights falling, cruel
voices calling, distrust on every
corner and purple mountains of
majesty lacking signs of Spring.
politics today is the long rattle of
hate, hearts of heavy stone and the
color of shame. politics is no laughing
matter when a rope taut around dark
necks is a forecast of democracy's
end.

NIGHT

I saw the sheet paper signs
on the street light posts on
First Avenue scribbled with
perfect english phrases, empty
beer cans leaning on stoop
steps and the faces of old
women watching from their
windows. I began to see Christ
nearer to the winos in the square
park passing around a pint of cheap
wine, the junkies wheeling and
dealing on corners, the patches
of clouds floating from West to
East and the white faces of the
newest colony of East Village
artists standing beside their work
displayed on sidewalks. I imagined
a huge flock of pigeons lengthened
in night flight, wondered if the moon
would come out to play and then
I turned the corner and walked the
block until coming upon a small garden
of flowers that appeared to urge me
to find what can't be seen.

SHOTS

we have entered another
night of empty prayers
offered by leaders with
mouths full of scripture,
hearts of stone and souls
owned by the NRA. after
the gunfire, the thoughts and
prayers of legislators will
again collide with heaven
for not doing a damn thing
in the law chamber to make
the madness end. for men,
women and children choking
on blood there is no blessing
in mere prayers, and there is
nothing left but apathy in a
democracy gasping for breath.
what good is prayer for those
who suffer and weep?

THE STORY

they came a very long way
to have their children born
in the great experiment run
today by mostly potbellied
old men that Whitman after
the fall of Lincoln wrote up.
they came to touch God's
english speaking altars, to
kneel in foreign language
spaces with souls scarred by
centuries of affliction. they
came to pray in the Spanish
made by the almighty and
hated by the english only
church. they came with hearts
filled with a book of stories,
under the cover of night and
supplied with words to name
the extensive list of sins that
built the White House. they
came to tell their children even
Jesus would have to learn english
as a second language in school
so gather every word you can in
your country of birth.

MOONLIGHT

many nights ago, staring into
the canyon made by buildings
motionless beneath a half-moon
aided by streetlights, we looked
over building tops saying prayers
and between them talking about
Spanish given to us by mothers,
a culture that stretches to places
existing before the invention of
America, memories of tropical
waters, a mythic forest singing
in pitch and a world needing the
tears that roll down our cheeks to
help it see. oddly, on the rooftop
no one tried to reduce things to
neatly package words or feelings
into the frail hands stretching out
to God in heaven.

WAITING

they didn't want to tell me the
story of the girl whose mother
came from Puerto Rico on a
winter day that froze her feet.
they didn't want to tell me before
Mass where people recognized who
made the world, were allowed to
speak Spanish and argued about
God forgetting how to answer simple
prayers. they didn't want to tell me
that Carmen Julia died too soon, her
precious young life ended with a
needle still her arm. they didn't want to
tell me they called out to heaven from
one side of the block to the other until
they were certain the death of this girl
was known by some God. they didn't
want to tell me they believed prayer
would make God take up their cause.
they didn't want to tell me how lonely
they felt waiting and waiting for divine
comfort.

RIVER BANK

I walked to the edge
of the river thinking
about the brilliantly
flawed ideas of ancient
thinkers like Thales who
held all things come from
water, Aristotle that frogs
are birthed by mud, and the
800 verse poem traditionally
named On Nature penned by
the philosopher from Elea. I
gazed long into the dark water
thinking perhaps nature does
speak to us in code like bees
that occasionally land in hair no
differently than when they gently
danced on Plato's lips inspiring
him to think math is the foundation
of reality though my illiteracy with
numbers will not confirm it. today, I
would like to believe light sneaks
into the world through our eyes and
hope goes out to sea to murmur wildly
in faraway places new songs.

JIMMY

in 1968, I learned to keep my
eyes open walking on Intervale
Avenue staring at falling leaves
from the sickly trees in the little
park. I recall thick clouds crossed
the sky in a hurry, and a colossal
darkness came over the block
when we learned Jimmy was
killed in Viet Nam only one month
after turning 18. he became just
another slain teen recalled with
praise by monuments in a world
he could not make any better. I
stopped shouting hosannas at the
years behind me and now wail
more for a world of bloodshed
and lacking peace. sometimes, I
think about Aeschylus who explained
that even in sleep wounds are not
forgotten, they spill into our heart
and sometimes wisdom shows up
thanks to a touch of God's "awful"
grace.

THE VETERAN

the veteran who lost a leg
visited his grand daughter's
8th grade class. in broken
english he told stories to kids
not once holding back a tear.
the boys and girls heard he
was afraid to brave foes in the
Southeast Asian jungle in a
war that belonged to the rich
who sent the poor to die. he
dragged haunted years around
with him and when veterans' day
returned each year questioned
how terribly inhuman was his
country in need of war gods to
bless every damn slaughtering
campaign.

PSALM 71

there are people on this block
who rush to factory work on
Bruckner Boulevard thinking a
wage will deliver them from the
hand of wickedness in the world
believing wonder no longer matters.
I watched them heading to petty
wage jobs, chasing the wrong God
the whole day long, and betraying
the infant hope that led them from
small village streets. I sat on stoops
whispering into morning spaces light
can never be lost in the dark and hope
in the barrio will always find ways to
to imagine it full of grace and touched
by the simplest and most delicate flicker
of redemption.

DARKNESS

waking in in a cheap
hotel room alone, castoff,
thoughts tumbling in your
head faster than the day you
ran from Tarzan chasing you
with a bowie knife and thinking
of the East River whose tide
rolled in and out of the invisible
life of street people. you feel the
chill in the darkness moving around
you, hear voices in the hallway of
the midtown hotel and you let your
tired eyes carry you back into a
deep sleep. you dream of the weary
trying to spot light falling at your
feet.

CERTAINTY

the thin skin of frost is
settling on the morning
surface of things. the chilly
time begins filled with tales
stretching from Mockingbird
Lane to Intervale Avenue and
pedestrians walk long streets
with shivers. each precious
second hides the forgiveness
leaning from heaven for the
people of these neighborhoods
desperate for signs. the words
of a Salsa tune burst out of a
window roaming sidewalks and
making their way to the river
becoming babble for penitent
ears. the cold wind does not permit
any to doubt their own existence
confirming the certainty familiar to
Descartes who lavishly doubted all
else.

THE CHILD

I have a problem child
with stories to tell and
problems to solve just
down the road in front
of us. I hesitate to speak
of her bitter times arising
to make us weep. though
our hearts will never turn
from love we drag long days
with weariness and the tears
clouding our eyes make us for
the moment blind to signs of
heaven. perhaps, you know
something of it, too?

THE LIBRARY

the pages on these shelved
books have folded corners,
some with faint pencil marks
eagerly sharing tales about
things in mysterious seasons
of life. I see a few books beneath
an arm on their way to circulate
in some other world with the
answers they keep for prying
minds that search. the oversized
book about La Virgen de Guadalupe
on a corner shelf has not been
opened in the last twenty years.
I walk the aisles slowing reading
titles I cannot wait to read. wooded
tables in this old library are close
to thousands of worlds and pieces
of paradise borrowers chase in the
stacks.

CLOUDY

a homeless elderly
man staggers across
an intersection with
a paper cup in his left
hand, a sidewalk table
plays host to a lunching
couple with a bottle of
Pellegrino. pedestrians
linger on the sidewalk
easing into the night and
a corner novelty shop plays
seasonal tunes with a few
muttering something about
dancing at Bethlehem and
hitching life to a star for
the sake of peace on this
tormented planet. I plan to
stand on the corner until
the three kings come riding
in from the East or until the
people they met on the road
cross the border with herbs
from their tiny villages for
gifts.

CHRISTMAS CAROL

windows were decorated
with stencil snowflakes
and colorful blinking lights,
and church bells are ringing
down the street. in alleys,
carol-singers rehearse hymns
for listeners rejoicing in the
advent season. Tito looking
out the window at the carolers
thought of the Dickens story
read in school about the elderly
man called Ebenezer Scrooge
visited by Spirits past, present
and yet to come. the English
story was one the little Boricua
boy loved for it takes the side of
a poor boy who knew something
of God and even more about the
hard labor his parents pulled. the
tenement windows were brightly
lit, Angels waited on the rooftops
and like the Christmas Carol tale
the earth seemed merry with peace
nearer to the earth and God's love
close.

FROSTY

the near winter sun
dresses the afternoon
with warm attire to
prepare us for a chilling
winter. the complicated
season will sleep the long
winter and we will wait for
different days like lovers in
Spring. when the first snow
arrives, we will listen for the
surprising words carried by
squalls, while making chubby
snowmen who will lean into us
under frosty stars.

DAUGHTER

I admire her for protesting
in womanish ways, a dear
daughter that tells me what
is wrong with a patriarchal
world, for wanting to build
a life where justice looks a
woman's way. I admire the
way she talks to other girls
about their rights in worlds
owned by men using words
to gag them, snatch freedom
from them and smother them
with their toxic masculinity that
pretends to know what is best
for the opposite sex. I admire
her strength refusing to feel
inferior, worthless, useless,
mindless and choked by men
in power who deny her civil
and human rights. I admire
her saying to the world, enough
is enough!

TIMES SQUARE

to the multicolored people
rushing about the sidewalks
on Broadway with more life
stepping off buses, dropping
from yellow cabs, and holiday
bright stores. to immigrants
dressed like Wonder Women,
Super Mario, Snow White and
King Kong frosting today like
a quinceañera cake and posing
for pictures. to tourists who
have come from far away and
stroll each night on Times
Square, weep in public at
the sight of the homeless,
laugh behind closed doors and
talk unintelligibly to baristas
about it being warmer back home.
to the delivery men on electric
bicycles approaching middle-age
with feint smiles, working for tips
and dreaming on rides. to all
embarking mornings into the
blue light of winter hoping to be
saved from the cold nights God
ignores.

REMEMBER

I remember kindergarten with
a kind white teacher who let me
draw clowns with tears rolling
down their cheeks and playing
78 RPM records in her class of
music never heard in the Bronx
tenements. I remember being an
altar boy in the Catholic church
where an Irish priest baptized
me, instructed me to receive a
first sacrament and played each
summer with the Puerto Rican
kids. I recall the Barbershop
where Joey's Uncle who learned
to cut hair in the Army gave us
crew cuts that lasted weeks, played
Salsa all day and who let us shovel
snow for a buck. I think of the Perez
bodega on the corner that sold
cigarettes to minors for a nickel
each, beer to old men who sat on
milk crates over a table top playing
dominoes, and the little kids who
played handball against the building
wall with pink Spalding. I recall
the widow who dusted Saints in the
church who told me she prayed for
us every day. I remember walking
home with Rudy one Easter and
finding fifty-dollars on the street
that I split with him. I think about

a first prayer in the dim light of the sanctuary asking God not to let me outgrow the fit of my only trousers. I laugh about the God who did not listen to my pleas, let me grow and finally offered a new pants!

ABANDONED

I lived alone in abandoned buildings
left by landlords that did not pay back
taxes, the doors were always open,
the windows boarded up, the wood
floors splintered and old linoleum
carpet pulled to pieces in what use
to be living rooms.   the junkies had
removed the copper pipes to sell for
a fix, old photographs could still be
found in bedrooms left behind by the
tenants who escaped to whiter sides of
town, and where I hung a rosary on a
nail driven into a plain ivory painted
wall given to me by a priest full of a
faith that strayed on the streets. I
settled my twelve young years in
such spaces to suffer the passing time,
shed childish baggage, and spend days
unlearning lessons about God and family
life. at night, I dreamt of home, going to
school and finding a way out of a shitty
world.

PERSPECTIVE

the little kids found out about
death in a borough of the city
the day a dog was crying with
its head out of the window that
opened too wide for the old lady
motionless on the sidewalk with
her greying hair-soaked red. they
discovered that death was like a
sheet of newspaper blown down
the street, the fire that turned a
whole tenement into ashes on
Simpson Street, the kites flown
on the rooftops that were allowed
to disappear at the end of thin lines
of string or the lost dogs roaming
the banks of the Bronx River who
bark death is forever. the little kids
looked at the limp elderly lady's body
pretending to know everything there
is to the unfortunate woman's end
and they coughed up lines from Father
Rossi who led the lightly attended
church. for lack of a better word they
called this another day to think about
religion making nothing happen.

CHRISTMAS

on a street that feared no
cops, on which a yellow taxi
had not been seen since the
last couple of white families
fled, and beyond the infamous
corner where Tito was chased
by a guy barely able to aim a
.357 magnum pistol to fire, the
tenement windows colorfully
decorated for Navidad played
a salsa version of Angels We
Have Heard on High. it was
two nights before Christmas
on the block, the junkies were
stirring, the old biblical scholar
Clement Moore's iconic poem
was being read on fuzzy black
and white television sets, los niños
were not tucked away en sus camas,
Lelo did not even own a pair of
pajamas and these little Boricuas
wondered would San Nicolas ride
in by sleigh or subway. they desired
to see the chuckling gordito, hoping
for gifts, perhaps dinerito, they just
wanted to be called by their beautiful
names Ay Papo, Ay Shorty, Ay Lefty,
Ay Cuca, Ay Nene, Ay Egita, Ay Nelly
Ay Rudy, and certainly hear "Merry
Christmas to all, and Feliz Navidad!"

PIETY

meditation they say is good
for you though taking an awkward
posture may be fully unappealing.
I prefer simple acts of breathing,
sliding along the sidewalk in a
noisy city, lounging on an old park
bench beneath a name carved tree,
waking from half-sleep to the sound
of birds singing their daily devotion
and finding thousands of reasons to
chuckle at the triviality of time for
the affairs of the living. I like to
consider with unique thoughts all the
temporary things experienced, the
magnificent clouds moving along just
below heaven to the sound of God's
voice and taking in the proud delights
of creation's symphony.

NUESTRA SEÑORA

Our Lady of West Farms Road
blessed like the little girl on the
altar in the church and the infant
in thy womb soon full of breath,
sending letters across the police
state border, visiting jail to see
your beardless son, clinging to
your Rosary with thin fingers
and holding a cup of café in the
other hand, prays for pecadores
like us running the streets. dear
Holy Madre hallow be thy name,
remember little Joey lowered on
Christmas into the earth, comfort
the men hanging in the parking lot
of the 7-Eleven looking for work,
give the migrant hating governor
a taste of your undocumented God,
bless the good works lingering on
earth and shine your big flashlight
eyes into the dark. Nuestra Señora
of junkies, thieves, muggers, coyotes,
prisoners, laborers, hambrientos, los
pobres touch those trying to figure it
out.

THE WALL

people who plead for
God's mercy have a thing
against walls made with
hate, thick with shame
and in a rush to keep
the ill-fated out. they
refuse to climb ramparts
to throw stones in vile
games and at night they
come out in scores to write
God tear down this abysmal
thing! I do recall a wall in a
concentration camp on which
a Jewish prisoner etched
if there is a God, he will
need to beg my forgiveness.
damn right! a wall is violence,
choice and a division raised
in front of many eyes on the
southern border to repel and
silence those who arrive still
wearing the river and every
scar produced by America's
sins.

SEASONAL LETTER

I write today this simple letter
though after years attending
church have no definite address
to which to send it. I hope you
have not changed too much in
the passing years, the boys and
girls you know are excited about
your birth and the wrapped gifts
it delivers to them. those departed
this year with different ages and
names are likely quite familiar to
you by now and are eternally in
waiting so forgive me for saying
this please do not forget them. this
morning people will march to a
church like shepherds, some on
snowy roads, others beneath the
warming sun, many hoping to see
your gracious light float into the
sanctuary from painted windows,
more than a few saying prayers in
the first pews certain they are very
close to you and everyone feeling
they are about to open the best gift
ever received. I ask you now to
keep us under the star of Bethlehem
until time comes to an end, work us
to your good and let us in ups and
downs not be afraid.

THE WALK

they have walked for days
many having never been to
the United States, eating bits
of village treats, gossiping
the things they already miss
about home, talking in the
tongue that is always ready to
speak whispering, crossing a
couple of borders in the last
month alone and anticipating
the final crossing before getting
to an english named street to
share a universe of secrets that
may one day answer the stiffest
riddles of America. in the light of
day the children pace toward the
big river, at night they are carried
by tired mothers who notice every
sigh of the wind, while the tired
elderly endure in the flesh this
northward march to find a place
that will not dare hide God's candle.
they are coming to remind us of
hope, the failures of a nation of
immigrants, the pain of the loathed
and things this nation never takes the
time to see.

LAMENT

I wept on Hoe Avenue the
night you were beaten on
the way home to a tenement
where not one miracle from
biblical days was experienced
by the people who began when
Columbus introduced a world
of hate. I roamed the streets of
two boroughs weeping on them,
whispering good-night to those
who ached, the poor girls whose
names remained a mystery, the old
men with sweated brows and the
corner of the room in the abandoned
building I knew for a home. as the
new year approaches, my eyes are
tired of crying for God's children
in a world ruled by greying men and
women of wealth that cheapens them
and keeps them in everlasting misery
until death. if God still weeps this is
a perfect time for the divine eyes to
get soaked for the lives pleading with
heaven from the edges of society!

DEUS, UBI ES

what is God in a world
without us, absent prayer,
speeches, and ears to whisper
words of love? what is God
without a Holy Mountain, no
souls to care for before birth,
beyond the idea of perfect love,
no stained-glass churches, pipe
organs playing sacred melodies
and waters to make tremble and
part? what is God in a world of
wars, societies heaving hate and
the rich breaking the backs of the
poor? what is God for those who
prefer the dark, others with tears
never dried and promises like unlit
candles on earth? what is God who
cannot see the question marks at the
end of the sentences uttered by the
first slave and everywhere since by
those hardly able to lift a voice to
speak hope? in this world dressed
so beautifully for death, come and
tell me.

NEW YEAR

today, clouds float playfully
over rooftops and on a busy
corner a musical group from
South America with panpipes
and hand drums sing. an ashy
moon is out early, time these
last few days of the year has
moved slowly and mortal flesh
imagines with dramatic longing
what comes next. the new year
will arrive with many dreams,
a fresh blank calendar for each
to see, memories retreating until
they weep and in all the shattered
cities hope waiting to laugh out
loud. soon, we will recall threads
of other years of life, wandering
far from home, perhaps the story
of the ark in the period before the
flood and maybe even an end to
the tribal laws keeping the world
in mourning. at the appointed hour,
answering to songs in tender hearts,
let us chant like lovers to search for
heaven on earth.

WAITING

I see them standing on
the corner waiting for
the break of day in the
new year, living in the
spaces where time is
flawed, just blocks from
the East River visited to
see morning light, longing
for a message that will lead
them to pull needles from
their skinny brown arms
and saying later to pale
pedestrians who were too
poor to move to other parts
of town. not one ever had
a passport in hand, hope in
them never fails to stomp
in the cold and when you
look deep into their dark
eyes you get a glimpse of
God within. tonight, they
wait and sometimes kneel
on the sidewalk though to
tie a shoe instead of taking
a pose to pray. with longing
only steps away from the big
church gates they anticipate
you see, something will arrive
this time, and paradise they
suspect.

THE SEASON

in the beginning was prayer
without end, the words for
every season, for times of
grief and others to laugh, for
a time to be born and others to
let go, for days to keep and
others to forget, for children
loved and others never meant
to keep, for times to drip and
others for the Potter's sacred
tears to rain. fresh like the first
breathe taken on earth the new
year has rolled in heightened
with life and for the moment
unable to make us utter a single
confusing promise. it will be
a time to spend the days, weeks
and months trying to understand
how to live without hearing Angels
voices sweetening the saddest days
of a world that has no certain name
for God.

LISTEN

I did not die like too
many friends on the
block taking with them
an ocean of secrets into
the South Bronx graves,
leaving me with years
of questions, more than
a dozen letters not sent
and knots in my throat
appearing at the oddest
times. in the evening,
kids played in flocks
long past ten o'clock, the
old ladies with wrecked
knees sat watchfully on
the stoop trying to recall
by telling stories about what
love means. I must tell you
city lights heal me more than
sermons in church aiming to
give a sense of life and street
kids help me skip each day
toward some secret Eden
where voices can be heard in
the wind and laughter in the
clouds.

POTOMAC RIVER

I walk away from the Capital
to the path along the Potomac
River, dodging the cars at the

corners, with a book on the
anthropology of religion and
old wounds, and tourists with

wide open eyes greet me like
offering a foreigner welcome.
here are University students on

the water sculling their hearts into
a frenzy in rhythm with a feint
whistle in the air and they are

making their way back to the
boathouse near lavish Georgetown.
I stagger more than a few steps

recalling that in this city a domestic
insurrection took place in the name
of a former and monstrous head of

state who symbolizes the second
lost cause and despicable symbol
of white sin. I think some people

want to see justice done and an
entire political party whose first
president acted to save the union

and emancipate the enslaved is
outraged about holding a criminal
who lost reelection accountable to

the law—there are even millions
believing this jackass could order
the killing of political adversaries

and like some king remain above
the law that would settle things
for any other citizen. a man who

pulled off so many crimes, shared
security secrets, sold information
to international leaders eager for

the American fall, fabricated a big
lie and stole national secrets is free
to enjoy life more than when my late

Brown faced brother at fourteen years
of stupidity was thrown into reform
school (jail) for getting into mischief

in a train yard, where he climbed into
a freight car packed with toilet paper.
with friends, they threw rolls of toilet

paper at each other and were tossed
in jail by white cops and charged with
theft. I pause to lean against a river

walk railing thinking kids will aspire to
be president now just to stand like the
imbecile above the law! America who

will cry at your funeral?

VALENTINE'S DAY

the day approaches known for its
sweets, unending whispers, lovers
in hand and friends sitting at sidewalk
cafes until their voices fade into the
novel memories of evaporated years.
I will take flowers and even a box of
chocolates to the cemetery headstone
that reads Swing Low Sweet Chariot
on Valentine's Day. in that space of
quiet breathing across the bay I will
remember hope that does not wither,
the coming and going of friends and
being together in love and gladness
without need of words. this coming
day that celebrates romantic love like
Chaucer dreamed, accidental meetings
and dearest friends will see us hanging
windchimes on the street corners to hear
ringing hymns that say we are each far
different in the absence of love.

SNOWY DAY

the snow is thin on the tree
tops and on this chilly day
a few birds have gathered to
sun. they take turns beating
their frosty feathered wings
to warm themselves and sing
to the quiet street. a few kids
are outside refusing to be hostage
to the artic blast that fell from
the sky and they are running,
sliding and tossing imperfect
snowballs at each other whilst
shouting names. branches on the
big tree across the street are bent
like Cuca who is the oldest lady
on the block with memories of
hot days spent home at the edge
of a rain forest. she watches the
kids play recalling the first time
she laced rented skates to glide
on ice in her new world where it
seemed clock faces indulged the
bliss widening her soul. it is cold,
light is beginning to fade in the late
afternoon, but no one denies there
is more life!

CATHOLIC SCHOOL

the anemic tree in the little
park had initials carved on
on its side placed there by the
young girls who attended the
Catholic school that offered
morning prayers that made the
city cry. five days a week they
walked by the sickly tree, saw
Hank the neighborhood wino
sipped cheap wine leaning against
it, waved to the old women who
leaned with smiles out of their
windows and filled the streets on
the way to school with spirited
laughter. when they passed the
Perez bodega they noticed a jar
placed behind a store window with
a note that said guess how many
coffee beans are in the jaw. Rosita
looked at her school companions
eyed the display and remarked all
of them, por supuesto, and then with
utter delight she howled. these girls
went to their Catholic School every
morning faithful to the prayers left
in their ears by mothers who were
new to the city and hungering for
good news.

AMERICANO

the first time in Central Park
after a long subway ride from
another borough I was called
spic and ducked a bottle thrown
at me. I wondered what these
Manhattan white boys wanted,
did they realize kids like me from
the Spanish speaking side of town
were no less American than them,
or that we attended Mass with mothers
who prayed to Saints with English
names and more than a few of these
women even had little American flags
for special holidays they placed on the
edge of apartment windows. the murals
on the sides of tenements in the Bronx
that had our names were not tagged with
the word spic, when the young single mothers
pushed strollers down the sidewalk they
looked at our names on the building walls,
smiling at the memories commanded by
each beautiful brown kid. I never stopped
going to Central Park, enjoyed time with
friends on the Great Meadow, and felt at
home.

THE VISITOR

the visitor who had grown
accustomed to travel came
with dreams that were then
quite young. he entered the
apartment speaking perfect
Spanish, new wrinkle lines
on his face, feeling welcomed
and eager to make plans for the
next two weeks that would shift
the years in him. there were miles
to roam in this eastern city, places
to see, words to rumor about the
many places known, deserts walked,
jungles where ruins stand to talk
about and lots of candles to light
in places freeing sadness. the visit
from the man who arrived from the
other side of life with a lined face
and chapped hands gave the old
apartment a new voice to whisper
in a foreign tongue.

BREAKFAST

we ate a loaf of bread
for breakfast seated on
a worn bench with cars
and buses screeching up
the Avenue. rush hour was
getting started, the street
was busy with determined
workers, joggers, dog walkers
and pedestrians who hungrily went
into Tom's Restaurant to crack
jokes with the short order cook
easy over eggs. I bet my friend
that the South Ferry crossing the
river was likely packed with
more than a few strangers from
New Jersey enjoying a buttered
roll with coffee and absorbed in
the morning news. he smiled.
we leaned back on the slanted
bench like two homeless kids
praying for warm sunlight and
waiting for a miracle to skip the
Penthouses on Central Park West
to find us.

FATHER

you were bound to the sea
since the day you sailed to
fight another country's war
and fighter planes left you
with a lesser leg. the days
you spent ashore a closet in
the apartment held tools for
fixing neighbors' televisions,
making single transistor
Dick Tracy radios for little
kids and waiting for God to
sit for dinner at the kitchen
table to ask your indigenous
Guatemalan soul forgiveness.
you left work at a banana plantation
paying twenty-five cents to Indians
for 14 hours of work and making
the United Fruit Company owning
more than forty-percent of the land
in your country richer. you told me
one day at Crotona pool that hope
looked like the sea to you, or the
different kinds of corn you knew
that offered village life, or the living
water of rivers where you once wept
without hurting. I did not know you
for very long and God knows there is
a great deal about you to protest but
you taught me something about how
to stay alive.

SWIMMING HOLE

the little creek travels
along its way pooling
up beneath the bridge
from which Puerto Rican
boys dive. you can see on
the murky water a couple
of railroad planks fastened by
clothesline holding the body
of a muddy Boricua like he
was just another thing of nature
in the vast city. today, the kids
laugh incomprehensibly when
suburban trains rush down the
tracks on their way to Grand
Central Station that receive people
who do not know anything about
what happens in places their eyes
will never see. these kids up to
their throats in the East River, a few
floating on their backs, others on
the banks shouting praises know a
thousand and one ways to balance
the reckonings of the fondest dreams
given to them by the single mothers
to which they will forever be tethered
like kites.

THE FUTURE

what if I told you there would
be no end to the perversion of
politics, the frightened days of
police battered Black citizens,
the drowning of Brown women
and children in the river between
wealth and poverty. what if I told
you there is very little interest in
weighty understanding, that too
many citizens think white makes
right, social storms will keep on
trashing the rules of law and the
idea of democracy is just another
name for godless empire. what if
I told you the lives of Saints are a
lot less Holy, churches are easily
distracted from love, elected old
men love having the violent last
word and hope is a thing dressed
with weighted boots and tossed
in rivers. what if I said the future
is ethnic voices with thick accents
calling us again to find lost dreams
and the roads leading to worthy
light.

.

SUNDAY

Sunday is a rest day reserved
for church some say on the way
to a piety session, when no one
should forget to pray, and everyone
swear to be a little better. Sunday
others say is when love sticks to
everything like winter snow, hope
puts on a fine dress, needles are
at last found in haystacks and a few
sit in pews waiting to catch a glimpse
of the divine. Sunday morning is time
for scripture to be opened by readers
in love with stained-glass windows and
reflective souls, for singing old hymns
as sunlight filters into sanctuaries and
congregations expecting God to arrive
at an appointed hour. Sunday is a day
to put on disguises while watching the
candles on altars flicker, to silence the
grieving, all hurt, insignificant Nazareth,
and a divided world. Sunday on this
shivering earth is boisterous devotion
to convenient truths that never get the
world right.

THE STENCH

the criminal defendant and
former president is flying around
the country eager to swim in his
swamps, sowing disharmony in
the name of a world darkened of
light and just like a bronze squirted
assassin with a rich Daddy's brand
name. America's first rapist former
president is a clear sign of the trouble
that happens to women, children, the
darker skinned, the global weak and
in the places human beings live where
empire has reached. the world's most
celebrated convicted felon has a crush
for global thugs like Putin, Orban, Jinping,
Jong Un, Hitler, and seasoned executioners
scrubbing their hands with innocent blood.
the fraud who believes he can shoot someone
on 5th Avenue without losing votes, hustling
mom and pop to pay legal fees, the GOP
nominee who is endlessly reckless and
entirely full-of-shit knows nothing about
human decency in the land of life.

THE WALK

we boarded the subway
jostling the ride downtown
to look for the carousel in
Central Park in search of
lovers riding it. the sun cast
warm light on the pigeons
claiming the trail leading up
to the magical wood ponies
spinning up and down in a
permanent circle. we saw a
few kids steady on saddles
spinning a world of dreams
on the merry go round but
we could not find a single
sign of lovers. we decided
to walk further along to the
lake where we found an old
woman on a bench who lived
off handouts and a couple in
a rowboat in the middle of the
pond embracing and with love
on full display.

THE BOYS

we went up to the rooftop
with the devil in a glassine
bag the evangelicals could
not identify. the junkie boys
were in desperate need of a
fix to calm the other demons
in them, to take the place of
street pain, forget the bullet
that claimed Papo's life and
the wicked one that detests
being alone. for some reason
these boys could not be found
by God who hung around in
the Catholic church on Hoe
Avenue, the storefront prayer
house on Intervale Street and
the Presbyterian assembly on
Home Street where the preacher
said God oversees all things. the
boys jammed a shared needle
into scars dressing their veins,
more darkness taking its place in
them and not even a visit to a
Holy altar would permit them
to swallow enough light to find
a way to say with the pious kind,
Hallelujah!

LOST

crying from the next door
apartment could be heard
up and down the building
steps. a chilly breeze blew
in from a broken hallway
window taking something
deeper with it down to the
street. the old men hanging
around the bodega waited
for it to reach them, but it
lost itself climbing into a
cross Bronx bus magically
stretching the wrong turns
of past years. I listened for
words to reach me from all
the tearful, thinking about
the edge of night and how
the people in the tenement
next door must have seen
the world to bring them to
such enormous weeping. I
have watched the darkness
come to us, the hunger, the
shootings, gang killings, the
battering cops, the endless
wars, the bleeding Black and
Brown faces and understood
the wailing in countless ways
belongs to us.

THE KIDS

smoke from the crosstown
bus on Saint Mark's Place
is released from its belly
covering the skipping rope
kids in blue. faces lean out
of windows taking it all in
and pallid faced youth with
punk dos are sprawled on the
steps of a Spanish speaking
church. University students
walk in groups on their way
to Washington Square where
the stars will cover their heads
and they will never think time
spins faster than the tops the
Puerto Rican boys on Avenue
D parade. on the West side, the
University constructs the Lower
East Side with books and the
screams of the kids growing up
junkies is silent like ashes from
a crematorium furnace. perhaps,
people with untroubled hearts
can make their way here to see
the wailing wall of this Alphabet
city that is too similar to the one
in Jerusalem.

THE CALL

last night the call came from
a small town beyond Detroit
where white college boys
explain the world looking
around to find dark-skinned
humanity to put down. all I
could do then was listen to
my son condemning Midwest
students impudently defining
who gets to be human. he wanted
me to listen to his objection to a
world rushing through him like
a demon setting fire to his brown
soul. I thought for hours recalling
the days, weeks, months, and years
of living in the same season of pain
in a different midwestern town ages
ago where it was often difficult by
the second to love my neighbor like
myself. we will talk again soon about
the history of our people that has danced
in his blood longer than recorded time
and I will remind him struggle-laden
human beings on this earth are like him
made in the magnificent image of
God.

FASHION

time marches a bit quicker
each year and the barrio kids who
have fresh memories of last year's
Easter in them talk about what to
do in a few weeks. a few of them
sitting on the stoop are sharing stories
of the wrong lies they told in school,
at confession and in the homes they do
not own. the good book they learned
to read in Spanish and English never
mentioned getting a new pair of shoes
and clothes for the high Holy Day when
Jesus according to the local spiritual
leaders comes back from the dead with
no regard for fashion. Tito was talking
about the half-snake shoes on layaway
in the fancy shoe store on the boulevard
to compliment the pepper silk trousers
the local tailor was hemming for cheap for
the big day. these kids hustled up money
shining shoes on the corner, carrying bags
of groceries for the elderly Jewish ladies
who gave tips and to put themselves in the
fashion barely ever seen in the sanctuaries
mothers cleaned weekly. soon, the barrio
kids would be all dressed up to get prayers
out of the way and roam the city displaying
their coolest threads.

FEW WORDS

this is my first letter to New York
with more than a few words rubbed
off the sides of buildings, some that
were spray painted on the number 2
subway and found late sitting on the
stoop listening to the music played
by the single mothers who hang out
on towels at Orchard Beech. I recall
roaming your streets, still have traces
of night chills in me, weep for dead
friends too many upscale residents said
were nobody, fall asleep at night only
to tumble into dreams that show me the
pale faces on the richer side of town that
insist the bitterness wrinkling them is the
fault of spics and people once property
deserving early graves. I confess there
are times when the light enters me like
Spanish words that guide me to beg God
for gracious peace before the world known
to me is even dust. I think somewhere on
a sidewalk, hidden in an old tenement, or
an alley holding disordered trash cans that
get rummaged by winos and dogs, the very
good that has escaped all the dark times
waits to be found. I will keep looking and
thinking about those who left us before their
time that you dear city promised would be
happy living with you.

LITTLE GIRL

in each Spanish word the
little girl took time to dance
to the sounds that called to
her from a place older than
her new home. with a smile
forming on her lips she knew
the meaning now of the words
on earth like in heaven and was
able to set aside the sadness that
threatened her apartment when
her mother kneeled before a simple
altar to pray. even then she dreamed
of counting hours until reaching
the day of not wishing for another
life.

LOVE

love is a thing more astonishing
than gates or walls darkening the
pages of the holy book. love is a
road inside the boundary lines,
the history wept by the poor, the
walk in a Spanish garden beyond
the terror of an English only world,
and making stops in the plastic tarp
dwellings refugees call home. love
is pure light living like a flock of
pigeons on Rachel's roof preparing
to wander in flight. love is naked
like an infant at birth, wetter than
rain, older than earth, deeper than
unchartered seas, not aching like
words, lush with forgiveness and
like corn a thing becoming people
who count eternity by life together
beneath stars. love is a thing like
adored incense, a pure cup of wine
and bread from the gods not one of
us will judge.

CONFESSION

no one answered the knock
at the door shut last night by
the family at church confessing
sins no newspaper would ever
print. the biggest violation was
caring more about being laid off
at work than God and how the
children already underdressed
for school would bawl for lack
of bread like demons straight out
of hell on Sunday. in the crowded
apartment they thought about tiny
changes to the world, finding Jacob's
ladder in the dim alley light startling
them to climb with Angels descending
from their ancient places to pull them
up with help from wings. the knock
on the door was never heard by the
people in the half empty centuries
old church that still talks about Jesus
walking on water to the family that
only a year ago walked across a desert
nearly dead of thirst. I cannot imagine
this family with its bundle of fear and
dreams differed having anything to
confess that will occupy the inattentive
ears of a God rarely moving about in
their world.

SLEEPLESS

I could not call last night
sleep when darkness came
in every shade to keep me
awake. you may agree even
the Psalmist finds time to
prowl dreams in the hours the
world is still and weariness gets
undone. yes, sleep eluded me
like rabbits dashing across a field
escaping noise startling silence. in
those night hours when no one has
hate, war nor violence in them, I
laid wide awake waiting for a divine
word to drift my way and set me
free.

THE PRISON

in the prison cell with its
peculiar silence you huddled
in the shadows tending to blows
given by those who want to
strike you down for claiming
innocence on a bitter day.
the place is stripped of clocks
for those who think your life
is like a miracle from heaven
though now in the stench of a
jail. the sun that rises has not
greeted your face for months and
the letters you write are saturated
with the language of sorrow that
aims to explain inmates who tape
pictures to cell walls of family on
the other side of bars, razor wire
and cages not meant for human
beings. tragedy wears a Black
and Brown face in this place of
mass incarceration filled with names
never mentioned in church. you are
a long way from making Sainthood
and I must tell you the martyrs are
siting up in their graves waiting for
you to be freed into the world Jesus
misses.

BOOKS

we walked eight long blocks
to the public school to open
torn books that have spoken
only english without talking
about the images paraded by
the Spanish Daily news of the
old Jewish lady that fell out of
her fifth-floor window, the thin
little kids that never heard about
eating disorders and the second
floor apartment in Papo's building
where six junkies were shot and
killed. we read lifeless books in a
school with classrooms filled with
Black and Brown faces and they
sometimes get carried to corner
stores, the little creek, a local Mass,
linoleum carpeted apartments or
the tarp residences on an empty lot
of Mapes Avenue. the churches
hold services too where there is a lot
of talk about what the repenting call
the good book, some even say it
is the book of books, though hustlers
on the block argue the old Bible is
a bunch of tales featuring nothing
more than God's mistakes with page
after page of barrio addresses crossed
out.

SWEETNESS

I love you since the day
you used little stones to
teach children tricks of
math on the dirt ground
by train tracks where they
settled. I love you in evening
dreams that wait for a new
morning with the moon still
in heaven shouting for me I
think of you. I love you as
you are with slender hands
that carry the cross for a Via
Crucis mass, for the simple
justice you pointed to without
permission in a country with
many crimes against the poor,
for weeping for campesinos
and believing paradise can be
found on earth. I love you for
lighting candles to the sacred
Mother and saying prayers to
her for the crucified who paid
for hope with their lives. I will
hold on to your tenderness and
welcome that fills me with bliss
on earth.

STILL VOICE

walking on the Lower East Side
one late Spring night, the news
shop on the corner receiving the
morning edition of what would be
yesterday's news, I could feel the
presence of a dead brother. he
had settled in my heart in a way
never like church the night of the
morgue visit on Easter eve to which
the cops called me to identify him.
my tears you see are made entirely
of him, this young man who was
imprisoned by pitiless streets, let
dope crawl in his veins and a liver
bleed Midnight Express wine until
a last sigh. there was no salvation
for him on Walton Avenue, no last
words left for the world, and no time
for him to look back with regret. he
lived a street life keeping him dressed
with thorns and on evening walks I
feel his world of hurt.

TWISTS

the liars who scream the
national anthem in public
space, those who spit at the
faces of the undocumented
and saddest in America, the
white pushers of hate and
swindlers in power are well
practiced in covering up their
crimes. they know just how to
burn disturbing evidence and
thousands of ways to declare
they alone belong in this country
with a slogan that says out of
many one. I recall the martyred
bishop who begged these very
people to see the world with eyes
that weep, to walk the stony roads
in the frayed sandals of peasants,
and to put bread in hands stretched
out on the church steps, the corners
and streets. perhaps, when the good
Lord returns from vacation these
forgotten things in the nation will
get sorted out.

MORNING

deafening traffic rushes
across the city to catch
tomorrow before sweetness
vanishes. I see lovers riding
a bus holding hands in the
lively morning secretly letting
out light. an elderly couple is
on the sidewalk not exchanging
words, strolling hand-in-hand
occasionally sharing a smile the
way one flesh is expected to do
without giving any thought to the
time of day or where they are on
earth. perhaps, no one knows
love like these companions and
I confess not tiring of peeking
in their direction to learn by heart
that tenderness is more than a season,
the counted hours, or memories
written on the finest paper intended
for gathering all the things owed to
the heart.

CRUCIFIXION

Jesus, sweet Lord, you know
on this land the poor are nailed
to the cross, dangled from trees,
tossed in shallow graves, burnt
in litter cans, tortured in bitter
places until killed and always
beaten down while people in the
church sleep. blameless child of
Mary, dragged away in the middle
of the night, betrayed by a kiss,
condemned by the pious who spat
in your face, sentenced to death by
hands washed clean, you know dear
Crucified God the people on this
land suffer, bleed, weep, and sag like
the two thieves on wood that do not
make the mighty tremble. sweet Lord,
do you hear the crying, will you carry
the poor's burden, split the Lilly white
veils in two, and give real aid to every
one who calls your name? darling Jesus,
please come quick before they murder us
again and again in your name!

MR. EX-PRESIDENT

the facts between the lines
are always there lurking in
and out of the reality that is
carefully manufactured for
the weary minds that have
been duped for centuries by
counterfeit tongues in power.
to people who are rendered
blind it is clear the unsaintly
politicians loathe the lovers of
truth, the opponents they smear,
the poor, the weak and citizens
who dare to weep. in this part of
the world, exposed tyranny has
been busily choking freedom to
death, therefore we must ask the
beaten, branded, silenced, and
slain about the propagandist with
a voice from Babel why the record
shows God has no use for him in a
future heaven knows he will never
own!

ROMERO

Romero had a message for
the poor who held too much
of the world's suffering. he
preached hope against hope
to them in the name of a
God of life who offered
comfort from a too distant
heaven. today, a Carmelite
sister met us with eyes filled
with grace and talked of San
Romero of the Americas who
was killed by a bullet that crossed
the border from the United States
shaped the image of death. she
recalled unremembered hours,
let us hear the martyred priest's
last homilies and leaned quietly
against a wall as the recorded
words of an Archbishop shattered
wretchedness still in us. today, we
sat in the space where Romero spilled
blood, the chapel from which his word
rang with love and his witness exceled
with freedom. today, we confessed
Romero's name clearer than the first
subversive brutally nailed to a tree and
promised to bear witness to his violence
of love.

THE WOODS

campesinos sit at the
base of a Ceiba tree
whispering to each
other the places old
bones are buried from
a civil war in which
rich rulers and cruel
dictators carved their
names in blood. they
sit quietly together still
weeping about a litany
of years made up of the
revolting voices that have
sickened them. they are
guilty of weeping for the
poor, daring to speak for
silenced voices, looking for
peace in villages, crossing
rocky rivers to escape the
end and regularly calling
on memories of love. tell
me what does it mean to
see elderly campesinos
sitting after the civil war
beneath a tree?

SPEAK

the sound of bells ringing
in the distance, children
running away from the
town square, the hideous
uniform of soldiers stained
by death, the desperate eyes
searching for the One they say
rose from the dead, the first
carpenter who made tables and
chairs nailed to the wood of a
tree, does make us wonder why
in a society shot full of holes we
believe. here are the places in need
of miracles, of joys to think, love
to feel and truth to tell, don't be
surprised if we wonder is something
worth saying about the shape of
things. Jesus, when will we stop
making this world so extraordinarily
wrong? will Lucifer's friends ever sit
on the wall to hear you shaking your
head about stolen land? the bells ringing
say it is time to stop white washing the
history of the world.

MEMORY

we talked with the people in
El Salvador who read poetry,
imagined the ways Jesus taught
his disciples in the hours that
wailed of an occupied state in
Palestine and recalling the poor
who resisted suffering, including
the soldiers who kill. we listened
to a story written by a Salvadoran
girl who is dead, prayed for her in
a valley that for too many families
remains a large grave and cursed
the land of the free that never gave
a shit. we listened to the witnesses
proclaiming someone should have
noticed the bloody village streets,
the children not playing, mothers
in mourning and the dark peasant
eyes escaping to America sodden
with tears. we have shared history
all these years, woke up each day
denying ghastly slaughters made
by Uncle Sam's dollars and without
light to see the Brown faces crying
stop!

TOUCH

I crossed to the West Side
of the street and you came to
the window speaking like the
forgiving Spring rain. I cannot
recall how often we held hands
into the evening talking about
an America that gathers the poor
and hungry on its shores and
the single mothers who cried
about still going with too little
bread. the world's best known
scholars of love have never once
wandered down these streets to
write of the tenderness made of
divine longing that would surely
fill the bookshelves of their very
fine schools. my thoughts have
dwelled for years on the sight of
Angels sitting on the edge of the
roof we swore to have grasped
and not even an unlawful clandestine
prison could keep me long from
you.

EL SALVADOR

in El Salvador, we walked stony
roads with those who knew too
much of evil and experienced
premature death making its way
down their throats until there was
no more than silence. we saw the
children in schools and villages dance
into the late afternoon on parched
messes of earth unaware of the open
wounds on their skin and the enormous
vulnerability that comes at the edges
of society that is demanded for them
by those gorging on their brand name
lives. In El Salvador, we learned more
about God than any seminary book ever
imagined, recalled with the poor the lives
of martyrs and though accustomed to think
differently met the Saints that were never
weary of standing for the truth. In this tiny
country, the propaganda posters cannot cover
up the bullet holes or the coffee cups filled
with the scraps of sliced campesino skin from
whom the people of the United States look
away though God sees.

FACES

underneath the faces
on the noisy streets
are those practiced in
love to be worn like
light in the dark. these
faces are carried with
a thousand dreams to
start new life.

SPANISH KIND

you have spent weeks in
this private University talking

of Brown V. Board of Education
without mentioning the Latinx

cases that were legal precedent
for ending school segregation

called Mendez V. Westminster.
Sylvia Mendez became the nine

year old Brown girl represented
by Thurgood Marshall expecting

social equality in education. you
are an expert in the classroom on

civil rights though you seem to
have forgotten that "white only"

meant separate water fountains,
the balcony in movie houses and

no entrance for Mexicans and the
"Spanish" kind in restaurants and

other white places of gossip. you
have never said a word about the

lynching of Mexicans in Texas,
the police who looked the other

way when white mobs kidnapped
Brown youth to dangle from trees,

nor have you condemned the racist
history tied to 'Operation Wetback"

that was responsible for the mass
deportation of Mexican nationals.

you consistently overlook the U.S.
government program in Puerto Rico

that called for the sterilization of
one-hundred percent of Puerto Rican

women in child bearing age, citizens
too of the United States! we belong

in America, carry dark skin like Jesus
in all the Juan Crow spaces, walk in

the places of senseless cruelty and
are the other language people in

the harvest fields, the meat packing
factories, the chicken farms, assembly

lines, cleaning crews, lawn care teams,
construction workers, domestic laborers

and also astronauts, teachers, lawyers,
athletes, doctors, artists, composers,

soldiers, even a judge in the U.S. Supreme
Court saying being Brown is not a problem

and will never be out of sight. let me say
you have never studied history unless you

admit you are nothing without your darker
kin—us!

VIDA

life unfolds each day
in the ways it knows

best with the graceful
sun strolling heaven over

the land until dark and
love is unfolded beneath

a starry sky with hands
held tightly and darling

softly whispered into ears
that guide this word into

a softened heart. what is
love after all if it is not you

wheeled across God's earth
and always far greater than

words.

ILLNESS

what can I tell you? she fell ill
unexpectedly with me rushing to
her side demanding to know why
God made the choice tonight not
to save? I suspect the God of this
mysterious world had no role in
your feinting spell nor the chilling
time when tears made their way to
the knots in my throat where they
were held back. in these few hours
of real life you slowly came back
into the world, while I pleaded for
the end of illness. you finally smiled
sitting up on the edge of the bed
where I held you and you looked quite
brilliant, again. we decided gently
talking that the God who made the
earth, tossed stars into heaven and
gave creatures this sweet life could
not know for whatever reason time
would come around with vulnerability
and the beauty that is always so very
impermanent.

.

DISAPPEARED

the night you asked me on
the block where have you
been, I confessed being a
boy who disappeared into
a world where trumpets do
not sound and God gave up
the earth to be wronged by the
sponsors of Banana Republics
who take turns dressing up with
the emperors old clothing. I roamed
across the land once in the hands of
fallen Indians, worked with the blood
of slaves, until invisible people living
in darkness took me by the hand. I
talked with peddlers in Mesoamerica,
lived stranded with merchant sailors
on a rock in the Caribbean Sea, looked
for signs from heaven like searching
for the certainty offered by daily sunrise
and nightly stars and experienced life at
the edges of society filling the church's
words with holes. I must confess living
many years thinking about the sorrow of
those who survived their dead, the people
discounted in any human tongue, and have
found peace in the company of peasants who
stared at bodies in shallow graves stubbornly
seeing paradise.

STRANGE

strange that we pray so long
to God without taking time
to find signs of heaven in the
beggar on the church steps,
the prophetic words uttered
by the poor in every season,
and the many human beings
that are fixtures in places at
peace and war. odd how we
dwell seated in church pews
listening to the timeless good
news with many things locked
up inside swearing about creeds
that offer empty threats about
righting crooked roads. strange
that many church windows are
stained with a white Jesus like
he existed in such color of skin
in the Middle East, was never
a refugee, poor and talked about
self-emptying love. Good Friday
approaches faster than the cries
of children who are facing misery
in Gaza and still the pious lot will
wait sentimentality for Easter easily
ignoring what Teresa de Avila made
quite simple, "Christ has no body but
yours."

CITIZENS BEWARE

the former president was speaking
after a reduction of his bond for a
civil liability of business fraud in
defense of his moral disorder, the
stupidity of admirers and the stone
cold capitalists who really think his
second term would make them just
a lot richer. with the flare of a serial
liar, the face of a carnival barker, the
man with a state secret tan once again
has demonstrated high crimes do pay.
he spat words into the air in front of a
courthouse foul enough to make Jesus
silent and too many look away from his
preparations to set fire to democracy like
a present-day Nero who allegedly burned
Rome. it is almost impossible to think of
a man who doesn't believe in truth, care
for the vulnerable, the rule of law or the
remains of years of bullshit lodged in the
back of his throat. I weep for the people
who died yesterday for him, those who
wrote their names on his wall, and the
countless to be trampled now that the old
liberty bell is paraded by the left and the
authoritarian mobs away from democracy
and made to slouch toward the malignancy
of tyranny.

FOR HEAVEN'S SAKE

we turned to each other in
the years not too long ago
when people dared rise up
against hatred and believed
in finding goodness. we often
stared down the dark, opened
our mouths to speak the truth,
knew where to find strips of
light, and listened to a world
speaking to Spanglish faces
saying, we will build the wall.
we gossiped on stoops and even
a few mountain tops about the
walls high in us, how they must
go along with the heresy of this
so-called Christian nation that
has turned away from the hill city
of Holy Jerusalem. more than once,
we said in the barrio here in dark
flesh is the image of God. we sat in
a church listening to the Book of
Revelation preached about a savior
not yet showing up and whispered a
a litany of woe overlooked by the
unemployed lynched carpenter that
many bow their heads to admit with
pious prayer.

GOOD FRIDAY

the ground beneath the
cross at noon is darkness
with horrified sighs from
a despised man lynched to
the wood of a tree for the
sake of human criminality
unsatisfied with every drop
of blood. the bang upon the
nails can still be heard in this
Good Friday world aching each
day to be set free. once upon
the cross you see we believed
the Word made flesh in death
would lead us all with love to
life. what do you say about
that greatest love that gave it
all especially for the least of
these, the sake of everything
and humanity?

JAZZ

I sat in the Village Vanguard
one evening to hear a Brazilian
jazz guitarist in the city for
the first time playing in the
pale light of a place that had
moaned more than any dared
to count. the musician conjured
a torrent of spells touching the
acoustic guitar strings creating
sounds not even Angels visiting
the Greenwich Village for a first
time could duplicate. he wrapped
the audience with the warm magic
I imagined God felt when breathing
us to life in a creation already laid
out with water, crackling sounds and
numinous beats. this guitarists for a
couple of hours introduced us to his
choir of heavenly spirits to which I
trembled with closed eyes saying this
is Jazz. the music rolled around the
large room when the bebop giant who
plays a bent horn, Dizzy Gillespie, sat
down next to me making me just about
hear the Latin jazz classic "Mas Que
Nada" featured in his Swing Low. Sweet
Cadillac" album. Man, everything came
into being in that basement in the village
around long before I was born and likely
there when I break loose!

THE CHILD

this child has eyes that can see
the wind, foxholes in the dense
woods and the love that gathers
to see her grow. we have photos
of her that whisper to each other
stories full of laughter and days
when a mother could do no more
than weep. you sit beside her in
joyful light with birds not daring
to fly sorrow outside the hospital
window and your heart like a kite
goes high to meet God. beside this
child, you stack wonderful stories
in all the corners of the room, hold
hands and feel the sparing seconds
of paradise on earth.

THE BLOCK

he walked home from the old
neighborhood with stories on
his hunched shoulders about a
kid put on the ground by cops
from the 41st precinct for spray
painting the names of the dead
on the telephone building wall
that sheltered the messages of
destruction sent around the city.
this boy was already tired of the
stained sidewalks before him, the
great disappearing act of a God
that had no servants on the block
and apparently had forgotten how
to lift the veil of darkness from the
brokenhearted. he carried with
him the memory of martyrdom, the
names of friends carried inside of
him scattered across the city to rest
in cheap cemeteries and pieces of a
black memorial cloth kept from the
day his brother was buried by the
Ortiz Funeral Home. no matter how
often his cries circled the big church
it could not get through the stained
glass windows warmed by the sun
and to the ears of the priest dressed
with fine leather shoes.

PIETY

I was thinking about telling you
when it all began in the barrio
with people snapping like dry
twigs underfoot, the Viet Nam
war claiming by way of a draft
the lives of Puerto Rican boys,
the sidewalks swallowing an
entire generation of children
strung out on dope that poured
into the neighborhood making
white old men rich on the other
side of the city and Anne's son who
was named Lazarus for damn sure
not coming out of his grave. John
Keat's would find no time here to
fear ceasing, no magic hand of chance
to keep him from next year's pleasures,
not even a paragraph of english words
to lyrically summon the beauty he held
most dear. I wanted to tell you a story
with words that take sides, gossip like
the widows in St. John's Church and
never condemn the Brown boys and
girls in a barrio full of these precious
human beings.

HIDDEN

tell me where the hidden dreams
are kept, the places where things
are put in their place and the dark
is attached to bright light. introduce
me to the little boys who painted
the meaning of life on the walls of
a building on West Farms Road
they forgot once the spray paint
can was empty. tell me where Joey
keeps the kites that pull clouds
across the rooftops in flight, let me
hear laughter from the saddest souls
on the block and the songs abuelas
sing at their windows that bend the
streets toward heaven. tell me how
to find rest for my heart laboriously
searching for a heavenly lullaby that
will direct to the very spot where Jesus
weeps. tell me is it the place where the
grass comes up from the cracks in the
sidewalk, wherever children are taken
by the hand to cross streets or in those
moments of lighting candles in the old
church that claims the Creator blind to
the block is not impotent.